HOW WOMEN LEAD

HOW WOMEN LEAD

8 Essential Strategies Successful Women Know

SHARON HADARY

LAURA HENDERSON

New York   Chicago   San Francisco   Lisbon   London   Madrid   Mexico City
Milan   New Delhi   San Juan   Seoul   Singapore   Sydney   Toronto

The **McGraw·Hill** Companies

2 3 4 5 6 7 8 9 0 DOC/DOC 1 9 8 7 6 5 4 3

ISBN: 978-0-07-178125-1
MHID: 0-07-178125-0

e-ISBN: 978-0-07-178124-4
e-MHID: 0-07-178124-2

This publication is designed to provide accurate and authoritative information in regard to the subject matter covered. It is sold with the understanding that neither the author nor the publisher is engaged in rendering legal, accounting, or other professional service. If legal advice or other expert assistance is required, the services of a competent professional person should be sought.
—*From a Declaration of Principles Jointly Adopted by a Committee of the American Bar Association and a Committee of Publishers and Associations*

Library of Congress Cataloging-in-Publication Data
Hadary, Sharon.
    How women lead : 8 essential strategies successful women know / by Sharon Hadary and Laura Henderson.
        p. cm.
    ISBN 978-0-07-178125-1 (alk. paper) — ISBN 0-07-178125-0 (alk. paper)
    1. Women executives. 2. Women in the professions. 3. Leadership in women. 4. Success in business. 5. Career development. I. Henderson, Laura, 1946– II. Title.
    HD6054.3.H33 2013
    658.4′092082—dc23
2012017097

McGraw-Hill books are available at special quantity discounts to use as premiums and sales promotions, or for use in corporate training programs. To contact a representative, please e-mail us at bulksales@mcgraw-hill.com.

This book is printed on acid-free paper.

Sharon dedicates this book to her parents,
Doris and Gideon Hadary.
They showed me nothing is impossible if I believe in it.

Laura dedicates this book to
her sons, Blair and Christopher Willcox.
There is nothing in my life they don't
touch and make better.

And to

Cindy Pearlman.
She has taught me the power of optimism and
the wisdom of seeking joy in every day.

Contents

Contents

Acknowledgments

For both of us, this book is the culmination of a lifetime of learning, experimenting, and figuring out what works and what doesn't. During that lifetime, there have been many people who have nurtured us in business and life, sponsored us, and generously shared their insights, knowledge, and experience so we wouldn't have to repeat their mistakes. Some were intentional advisors, and others influenced us without even realizing it. To everyone who has been part of our life journeys and made us who we are, we thank you so much.

The path to publication is filled with serendipitous coincidences and intentional planning. A great number of people touched our lives during this process—sometimes we reached out to them, and sometimes they just showed up in our lives at the right time.

It all started with three people we had known for many years: Dr. Gwen Martin, Juanita Weaver, and Bruce Rosenthal. Their long-term encouragement, support, and connections made this book possible and made it much the richer.

Then Tamara Monosoff and Lillian Lincoln came into our lives and shared their experiences as authors so we would know what to expect and how to avoid the potential pitfalls.

We even enrolled our families. Laura's son Chris Willcox read the manuscript, asked us probing questions, and cleaned up our writing. He has been as committed to the success of the book as we are. Sharon's sister, Susan Hadary, advised us on branding and marketing.

Along the way, both longtime friends and new friends came into our lives exactly when we most needed them. Richard "Dick" Falcone read our manuscript and helped shape the final book. Eve Benton, George "Jug" Courlas, Becky Eason, Hope Eastman, Lee Frederickson, Marie Friedman, Sandy McDougall, Ellyn McKay, Eric Organesoff, Susan Peterson, Sharon Pinder, Bob Rosen, Detta Voesar, and Susan Wranik brought us connections, provided insightful advice and guidance, and encouraged us along the way.

There were a number of highly successful women business owners and leaders whom we interviewed for background knowledge. They gave us powerful insights into what it takes to be a successful leader and encouraged us at every step. Our thanks to Jennifer Bisceglie, Faye Coleman, Kathleen Diamond, Judy Penski, Kathy Smith and Kara Trout. Your insights, vision, and enthusiasm influenced this book more than we can tell you. Megan Pearlman added the perspective of a young, rising leader.

Special recognition must go to our agent, Jessica Faust, who believed in our vision, taught us about the publishing business, encouraged and advised us, and kept us going.

At McGraw-Hill, we are fortunate to have our diligent and capable editor, Stephanie Frerich, who has shepherded our book through the process, and the talented editing team headed by Scott Kurtz.

The book would never have made it to the publisher without the technical and administrative support of Elise Dearborn and Abby Lindberg. These two young women are future leaders.

Although Laura's friend and mentor, Jack Rennie, is no longer with us, the lessons he taught us and his enthusiasm for life and business are reflected in everything we have written.

The Women Leaders Interviewed for This Book

We especially want to thank the 15 women who believed in our project, took time out of their very busy schedules to talk with us about what they had learned about building a successful life, answer our follow-up questions, and cheer us on.

Kathe Hicks Albrecht, Visual Resources Curator, American University

Maria C. Coyne, Executive Vice President and Consumer and Small Business Segment Head, KeyBank N.A.; Member, Executive Council, KeyCorp

Debra Hanna, Associate Director, Critical Path to TB Drug Consortium at the Critical Path Institute; former Senior Principal Scientist, Laboratory Head, and Project Team Leader for Antibacterial Research at Pfizer Worldwide Research

Susan Helstab, Executive Vice President of Marketing at Four Seasons Hotels and Resorts

Beverly A. Holmes, Founder and CEO, B. A. Holmes & Associates; Retired, Senior Vice President, Retirement Services Division at MassMutual Financial Group

Marilyn Johnson, Retired, Vice President, Market Development at IBM

Diahann W. Lassus, CFP®, CPA/PFS, President and Chief Investment Officer at Lassus Wherley

Monica Luechtefeld, Consultant at Office Depot; Retired, Executive Vice President, Global E-Commerce and Direct Marketing and Member, Executive Committee, Office Depot

Camye Mackey, Vice President of Human Resources at the B. F. Saul Company Hospitality Group

Nina McLemore, Founder and CEO of Nina McLemore, LLC; former President and Founder of Liz Claiborne Accessories; former member of the Executive Committee of Liz Claiborne, Inc.

Kathleen (Kate) A. Nealon, Non-Executive Director at Argo Group International Holdings, Ltd.; and retired Group Head of Legal and Compliance at Standard Chartered Plc.

Usha Pillai, PhD, MS, PMP, Founder and President of Aria Management Consulting, LLC; former Senior Director at Pfizer

Kim Roberts, Director of Government Analysis at Science Applications International Corporation (SAIC)

Judith (Judy) D. Robinson, Colonel, Medical Service Corps of the United States Army

The New World of Women's Leadership

Sharon's Story

I still remember the instant I recognized that, as a woman, I was bringing a different perspective to the workplace, and that what I brought was valuable, insightful, and made a difference. It was the mid-1970s, and I was a second line manager in IBM's Federal Systems Division.

To put the situation in perspective so you will understand why this was such an epiphany and such a risk for me, I have to describe the times. In those days, women managers were a rarity. There were two or three women in senior manager positions in my division—mostly in the technical areas—and none to whom I reported.

My only role models up to that point in my career had been men. I had been one of only two women in my master's degree program at the School of Industrial and Labor Relations at Cornell University. It was me and one other woman among a class of 30, and all my professors were men. My first job out of graduate school was with AT&T Long Lines, where I was one of the first two women ever to be hired in the management training program. When I moved to IBM, all the successful managers I met and worked with were men. I did not know any way to lead but the way I observed these successful managers—all of whom were men—leading. As a result, I adopted men's leadership styles, learned how they made decisions and followed suit, and accepted their values in business as my values. The few books written for women entering the business world warned us to avoid managing like a woman.

It was a Tuesday morning. I was scheduled to discuss a personnel situation with my director. As I did on my morning jogs, I prepared for my important meetings that day. I played out the meeting with my director in my mind, from entering the office, through the discussion, and to the end, evaluating my arguments and key points from a business point of view.

I knew what would be considered the "right" decision—the employee should be fired. Yet, as I played it out in my mind, I wanted to argue to save the employee, to strongly advocate that firing him was not in the best interest of the company. "Don't be silly," I said to myself. "That's just a woman's point of view."

I can recall the epiphany as if it were yesterday. "But," I thought to myself, "I *am* a woman!" And I believed my woman's analysis was, in fact, the best strategy for the company as well as for the employee. At that moment, I consciously began to recognize and value the different perspective I brought to the business.

I took the risk. I built the business case in my mind for not terminating the employee, took a deep breath before going into the meeting, and argued my case. To my total amazement—and delight—my director agreed.

Happily, my recommendation turned out to be a good decision. We saved the employee, and he contributed to IBM for many years to come. After that, I became aware that in many ways, I managed people differently from my men colleagues. In addition to looking at the numbers, I added personnel and organizational considerations to my business decisions. I realized my success as a manager was in great part due to the added context I brought to decision making. My teams had always been highly committed to achieving our goals, and I realized this was one of the reasons—before finalizing major decisions—I had already considered the impact of the decision on my teams and usually had consulted them. Most interesting, I noticed my director began to make me his informal sounding board on decisions affecting our business unit, asking about what impact I thought the decisions would have and how the decisions would be received by employees as well as the internal customers we served.

I also realized that the way to gain acceptance for recommendations that were different from what management would usually decide was to present the recommendations in business terms. In this case, I had included the corporate investment in training the individual, the value he had brought to the company over the years, and the projected value of his future contributions to the company. I made certain to acknowledge the potential risks and included what we would do to minimize the impact of the risks.

After that, as I traveled around the company, I made a point of meeting and getting to know women managers. I observed them in meetings and followed their careers. I noticed that the highest-level women were hungry to discuss their leadership styles and how they were dealing with the challenges of being women leaders in a predominantly male environment—both to exchange information and to gain affirmation for their styles. So began my journey of studying how women lead, how women overcome their challenges, and what women have to do to assume their place in the top echelons of business leadership.

Fast-Forward to Today

Four decades later, it is a new world for women in business. Women moved into business at an unprecedented rate over the last 40 years, and by 2010 represented almost half the talent pool available to the United States and other economies. Their credentials surpass those of the men. After years of lagging men in education, women now have surpassed them in educational achievement—earning 52 percent of all bachelor's degrees and 60 percent of all master's degrees[1]—and are more likely than men to graduate with honors at both the undergraduate and graduate level.

The transformation of the face of business is particularly evident in the movement of women into leadership positions. Over half (51 percent) of all managerial and professional positions are held by women, more than triple what the rate was back when Sharon started in corporate America.[2] Women are moving into the levels of leadership where they influence strategy and drive organizational direction. The number of women corporate officers nearly doubled between 1995 and 2011,[3] and women's presence on corporate boards grew to almost 16 percent in 2011.[4]

For the first time in history, we are seeing women in corner offices, on boards of directors, in command of military units, holding high elected offices, on the floor of legislatures, and owning large businesses. Women are no longer as likely to face the challenge of being the "first" woman or the "only" woman. There are now role models from whom women can learn the way women manage and discover what works and what doesn't.

The movement of women into the workforce is having a tremendous economic impact. McKinsey & Company, an international business consulting firm that has been a leader in focusing on the value of women in the labor force, estimates that America's gross domestic product (GDP) is about 25 percent higher than it would have been without the influx of women.[5]

We now have solid studies that prove that corporations with women in leadership positions are surpassing other companies in profitability. In the last few years, headlines around the world have proclaimed the impact of women in leadership on corporate results: "Link between Women and Corporate Profitability," "Gender Performance: A Corporate Performance Driver," and "Firms with More Women in Charge Faring Better in Economic Crisis." For the first time in history, there is research showing that companies with more women in high-level positions report better financial performance than those with fewer women at these levels.[6] The results are astounding.

Pepperdine University researchers found that the 25 Fortune 500 firms with the best record of promoting women to senior positions are as much as 69 percent more profitable than the median Fortune 500 companies in their industries,[7] statistics critical to success on Wall Street.

Catalyst, a nonprofit organization focusing on the advancement of women in corporations, found that the companies with the highest representation of women in top management achieved a 35 percent higher return on investment (ROI) and a 34 percent higher total return to shareholders than those with the lowest representation. [8]

This is a global phenomenon. A worldwide survey of more than 100 companies showed that, regardless of national culture, companies with the most women in senior management reported higher operating margins. These companies also ranked higher than other companies on key performance dimensions: leadership, motivation, coordination and control, direction, and work environment and values.[9] These are areas where women's leadership styles are most likely to have an impact.

Studies in France, Vietnam, and Australia add to the evidence by documenting that companies in these nations with more women in leadership fared better during the recent economic crisis. These findings make a compelling business case for the value of women's contributions to organizational performance, and the business world has started to take note of this. Almost three-quarters (72 percent) of corporate executives in a recent global survey said they believe there is a connection between a gender-diverse leadership team and financial performance, up 12 percent from the previous year.[10]

Furthermore, women are making a difference by managing their way. As more women moved up the ranks, they began to recognize and value their innate leadership styles. They learned they could achieve results as good as or better than those of their male counterparts by taking a holistic view of management issues and operating with an inclusive and collaborative style. Top executives increasingly say these characteristics are critical to corporate leadership in today's global, fast-moving business environment.

Both women and men increasingly are recognizing that women's leadership styles differ from, and complement, men's styles, resulting in stronger organizations. It is not that one leadership style—male or female—is better. The greatest success occurs when the leadership styles of both men and women are combined. No longer should the discussion be which style is better; rather, the discussion must be how we can most effectively integrate the two styles.

Euphoria Gives Way to Frustration

For a time, it seemed that women had established an unstoppable momentum and were moving up the corporate ranks with alacrity. But in the last few years, women's progress has slowed. Despite the substantial evidence of the value that women bring to business leadership, their upward movement is not matching the rate of their overall movement into professional and managerial positions. Women get to middle management and stall. The growth in the numbers of women in executive positions and on boards of directors has remained flat over the last few years.

Adding to the frustration are new findings from Catalyst. Despite the positive images of women in corporate leadership tracks, a study from Catalyst found that women worldwide still are not advancing through the pipeline at the same rates as men, even when they have identical credentials, including MBA degrees. Most discouraging was the finding that around the globe, from the very beginning of their careers, women receive lower salaries and benefits than men, even when their backgrounds and education are the same.[11]

The salary gap only increases as women move into the C-suite. In 2008, the highest-paid woman executive on *Fortune* magazine's list of the "50 Most Powerful Women in Business" earned 11 percent of the highest-paid male executive; in 2009, it was 38 percent. In 2010 and 2011, the highest-paid woman executive earned about half what the highest-paid men did.[12] Don't think the improved ratio of women's to men's earnings is good news. It is not. During these four years, the women's compensation stayed relatively constant—it looks better only because men's earnings declined drastically, most likely because of the recession.

The System Still Needs Fixing

Many will say it is just a pipeline issue. "It just takes time." However, at the current rates, we estimate it will take women five to eight decades to achieve parity. That is just too long.

We asked ourselves, "What is holding women leaders back?" Clearly a key challenge is the mindset of most corporations. Despite the finding that almost three-quarters of top executives believe having women in leadership strengthens corporate performance, when asked what they were doing to advance women, most had not taken any specific actions. Companies have been slow to address the 24/7 culture, in which long hours and frequent travel are key to being viewed as high-potential executive material. They have been reluctant to introduce work arrangements to accommodate women's desire to integrate professional and personal goals and responsibilities, and when these arrangements are available, the perception of those who choose to use them is often negative.

Senior corporate executives and CEOs assume that compensation, recognition, and promotion policies are ensuring equality between women and men. When the Catalyst study documenting disparities in advancement rates and compensation was released, CEOs of Catalyst's member companies were among the most surprised. James S. Turley, the chairman and CEO of Ernst & Young LLP, is quoted in the report as saying, "Frankly, the fact that the pipeline is not as healthy as we'd thought is both surprising and disappointing. Companies have been working on this and I thought we'd seen progress. . . . This is a wake-up call for corporations . . . we need to make sure they're (women) getting the same development and visibility chances as the men."[13]

Women Won't Wait for the System to Fix Itself

While many corporations are introducing cultural and organizational changes, these systemic changes have proven to take time.

The issue of what corporations need to do to take full advantage of the power women bring to the workplace is being widely addressed in many forums today. High-profile business publications such as the *Wall Street Journal* and *The Economist* are sponsoring conferences and producing special sections in their publications to highlight the challenges and report on proposed solutions. But actual progress continues to be excruciatingly slow.

It is not in women's nature to sit back and wait until someone else fixes the problem for them. Years of research have shown us that when women are confronted with a challenge, they roll up their sleeves, take charge, and fix it. Based on our research and experiences, we see that the women who have risen to senior levels in corporate America took matters into their own hands, combining their female strengths and their understanding of business strategies to attain their positions. From these women, we learned that there are actions every woman can take to open up doors for herself, creating change one individual at a time. And, just as the women who led the way in the past initiated positive change and created credibility for today's women, the women who are moving forward today will open doors for other women and will contribute to accelerating the pace of systematic change in the corporate world.

Research has proven time and again that women have the capacity to be leaders and contribute significantly to profitability and success. All women need is the knowledge and tools to capitalize on their skills and strengths within the context of the business world. We believe women's potential contribution to business leadership is enormous. In fact, Goldman Sachs, an investment bank, has calculated that closing the gap between women and men in the workforce would increase the GDP in the United States by 9 percent and in Europe by 13 percent.[14]

Why We Wrote This Book

The women who make up the business pipeline are talented, motivated, and resilient. As we studied the challenges confronting women in leadership today, the two of us knew that our years in the business world and our research-based understanding of how successful women had overcome these challenges have given us valuable insights that need to be shared.

This book brings you the insights, experiences, and advice that we have learned from women who have made it. Through our work, we have identified specific, practical actions that women can take to build on their female strengths and achieve their goals. You will learn what differentiates the women who have been successful in reaching the top from those who have been less successful. We will share these insights in a practical yet inspirational manner to help you, as a woman, move through the pipeline at the pace you desire.

This book is for you if you are already in the leadership pipeline and want to move faster or more easily. It is for you if you are just launching your career and don't know what to do first. And it is for you if you are just beginning to ask questions about what you want to do with your life.

If you are mentoring or coaching women leaders, this book can be your guide to advising and supporting the women you are mentoring. It can be your gift to them as a blueprint for building their competencies and confidence.

What We Bring to the Table

We, the authors, are researchers and practitioners. Between us, we have spent years as leaders growing organizations. We have conducted research on women's leadership and studied the research of others. In addition, we have lived the life—both in corporate America and in the entrepreneurial world. We have experienced the journey to develop a personal definition of leadership, and we have had the opportunity to watch firsthand as our female colleagues took their own journeys. We have seen what works, and this book is our first step in sharing this with you.

Sharon has been a leader in creating social change for women for over four decades. She has been a corporate executive, a researcher, a consultant, a teacher, and an entrepreneur. When it comes to women's leadership, she knows the people as well as the data.

Sharon spent 20 years at IBM in personnel, management development, and communications and public relations. She was the founding executive director of the Center for Women's Business Research, which she built to become the premier nonprofit research institute focused exclusively on women's entrepreneurial leadership. She is credited with harnessing the transformational impact of data to alter the landscape for women business owners forever in terms of access to capital, markets, expertise, and networks. She has received numerous awards recognizing her contributions to women's entrepreneurship and women's leadership.

Today, in addition to speaking and writing on women's leadership, Sharon is an adjunct professor in the doctoral program at the University of Maryland University College. She serves on several women's advisory boards, is on the board of trustees for the Wisconsin Union at the University of Wisconsin, and is actively engaged in civic leadership.

Laura is an award-winning entrepreneur, speaker, and author. She is known for her innovative management style, her role as an advocate for women in business, and her active participation in public policy on the national, state, and local levels.

At age 32, Laura left corporate America to found Prospect Associates, a highly respected health communications and biomedical research firm. She grew Prospect Associates to over $20 million and nearly 200 employees. She was a pioneer in developing and advocating for management styles based on women's leadership styles and has been active in women's business issues for more than four decades.

Laura has a reputation as a business innovator and philosopher, fascinated by the endless opportunities for women's success. She has served on and chaired economic development councils as well as both nonprofit and corporate boards. She has received many awards for her business leadership and her contributions to women's leadership.

In 2000, she sold Prospect Associates and founded Henderson Associates. Today, she continues to serve on boards, consults on strategy and business issues, and is an active philanthropist. Laura maintains a strong sense of personal and family priorities. She has two sons. Her older son is an energy conservation engineer, and her younger son is an artist and author working in the field of neuro-science.

Both of us have had the privilege of working with all the players—women and men leaders from all arenas (corporate, entrepreneurial, and nonprofit, as well as policy makers, educators, and researchers).

In light of current trends, we believe there are three important questions:

- What differentiates those women who have attained top leader-ship positions?
- What can women who aspire to reaching senior leadership roles and to being the best leaders they can be learn from the experi-ences of these women and from the research we have conducted?
- How do we close the gaps?

So we joined forces to distill our experiences and research into a body of knowledge that answers these questions. We combed through our own 20 years of research with thousands of women leaders, added in the latest research on women's leadership, drew upon our personal experiences, and interviewed women leaders. What emerged from the research, interviews, and our personal observations was that the women who have achieved the top levels in business, nonprofits, and government have much in common. Equally important, we found that there are consistent, observable, and substantive differences between the women of achievement and those who have not achieved the same levels of success. This book is the result of more than two decades of study, observation, and practice.

In addition to our many years of research on women leaders, we interviewed 15 women leaders specifically for this book. They come from a wide variety of fields—banking, technology, office supplies, hotel management, pharmaceuticals, law, and the military. We asked them about their journeys, about the accomplishments that are their greatest source of pride, their challenges and how they overcame them, what they know now that they wished they had known earlier in their careers, and what advice they would give to other women. Most of them have children, many are married, and a number have been single parents for much of their careers.

Despite the diversity of their industries and backgrounds, there was an amazing consistency in their responses. Their journeys were not always easy—they encountered barriers, stereotyping, and nay-sayers along the way. They juggled family, personal, and professional goals, learning to integrate their personal and professional lives by establishing priorities. They set high goals, developed confidence in themselves, and established a foundation of values to guide their personal and professional decisions. They built professional and personal networks to expand their horizons and get the support they needed. They saw connections and possibilities where others did not, and they created new ways of doing business. Most of all, they look back with a sense of pride in their accomplishments and look forward with a sense of anticipation for what comes next.

Throughout the book, we illustrate key points with quotes and stories from these talented and successful women. When we use their stories and quotes, there are no footnotes to show the source. Instead, we have created a special section at the end of the book where you can learn more information about their careers and journeys.

In addition to the women we interviewed *personally*, we collected published profiles of successful women leaders, listened at conferences featuring the most accomplished women executives, and followed leadership blogs, especially those featuring women leaders. Throughout the book, we share with you the experiences and insights of these women as well. When we use quotes and stories from these sources, we have included footnotes so you will know the source of the quote and be able to find the published stories if you want to know more about the women and their careers.

The Eight Success Strategies

No matter how we approach the question of what it takes for women to be successful in business—through questionnaires, case studies, interviews, or observation—a consistent set of eight strategies emerges. Time and again, women attribute their success to having mastered these strategies. When asked what advice they would give other women, their advice also falls into these same eight strategies.

The eight essential success strategies are as follows.

Success Strategy One: Empower the Woman Leader Within

Success starts with empowering the woman within by recognizing, valuing, and practicing the leadership strengths that you as a woman bring to business. Success Strategy One gives you the knowledge to identify and benefit from your female strengths to achieve your full leadership potential.

Success Strategy Two: Own Your Destiny

Define success in your own terms based on your values, passions, and vision. Success Strategy Two gives you the tools to achieve that success by breaking free of the unconscious boundaries created by cultural expectations, by believing in yourself, and by setting high goals.

Success Strategy Three: Be the Architect of Your Career

Acquire the credentials for success. Success Strategy Three lays out the basic business experience that is essential to moving into senior leadership, and identifies options and opportunities to demonstrate your capabilities and accelerate your movement through the career pipeline.

Success Strategy Four: Advocate Unabashedly for Yourself

Be your own best advocate. Success Strategy Four shows you how to build your personal brand; to create the business case to position yourself as the candidate of choice for opportunities, recognition, or compensation increases; and to create a powerful network of sponsors, mentors, and colleagues who will be the wind beneath your wings as you build your career.

Success Strategy Five: Translate the Stories Numbers Tell to Drive Strategic Results

Set a high priority on developing financial acumen. Learning to read the stories that numbers tell is essential. Success Strategy Five provides the knowledge to become financially sophisticated in business, to understand how to follow the money, and to value building business wealth.

Success Strategy Six: Create Exceptional Teams

Leaders mobilize exceptional teams to achieve visionary goals. Success Strategy Six is your guide to applying your leadership skills to build high-performing teams and task forces, whether you are the leader or a team member.

Success Strategy Seven: Nurture Your Greatest Asset—You

You are your own greatest asset. Success Strategy Seven gives you the tools to transform your mindset from that elusive concept of balance to skillfully integrate your professional and personal life, to invest in yourself to be the best you can be, and to focus your personal time and energy, and to value building the personal wealth to live the life you want.

Success Strategy Eight: Turn Possibilities into Reality

Make a difference and have fun. Success Strategy Eight lays out strategies for how to reach a hand out to other women, use philanthropy to drive change, and stay open to serendipity, the unexpected opportunities that bring joy and meaning to our lives.

Empower the Woman Leader Within

As pioneers in women's leadership, we frequently are asked to describe the difference between women's and men's leadership styles. The early studies comparing women and men business leaders declared there were no differences—yet many of us realized that we were leading differently. How could these studies be right?

They were right because they looked only at basic business skills that are the backbone of any business leader regardless of gender, such as finance, planning, and operations. Every individual who is going into business needs the same basic mastery of what it takes to operate a business successfully.

What these early studies failed to consider is the style in which the leader makes decisions, creates teams, builds relationships, and leads people. That is where the differences are. Women create a different context around leadership. They are more holistic, collaborative, inclusive, and consultative than men. Today, we realize that these qualities are strengths that add to the success of the enterprise.

Testing the Waters

As more women moved into management, both managers and employees started to recognize that the approach that women bring to addressing business operations—evaluating situations, establishing goals, and solving problems—is different from that of their men counterparts. At first, this difference made people a little uncomfortable—not only the men in leadership and the employees, but even the women themselves.

It has taken time for women to feel confident leading in their own style. Their first attempts to manage differently were tentative. As they began to realize there was strength in their leadership style, they began using it when they managed their employees—managing down in a holistic manner, while maintaining their masculine approach to leadership when managing up.

When Sharon was a young manager at IBM, she got her first glimpse of how women lead differently. There was only one woman senior executive in the Federal Systems Division where Sharon worked. This executive always treated junior employees with consideration and respect, greeting them whenever she encountered them in the hallways or in meetings. This style was a very different style from that of the male senior executives. "She made us feel valued—even if we did not work directly for her," recalls Sharon. Many years later, Sharon heard this woman leader speak at a conference on women's leadership. In her presentation, the former IBM executive declared that she led in the same style as the men while she was at IBM. After the presentation, Sharon spoke to her privately about the difference between what she had said and what Sharon had observed. "Yes, with employees I was different," she said, "but when I managed up, working with my colleagues and bosses, I managed just like they did."

Become Confident Leading Like a Woman

Today, as we discussed in the introduction, there is ample proof that women's leadership styles are a valuable complement to men's leadership styles. No longer are women managing down one way and managing up in another. Women are gaining the confidence to manage in a style they recognize is both authentic and effective. Men are realizing that having a woman's perspective adds insights that lead to more effective decisions.

Many people would like to proclaim that women lead better than men. This statement makes great headlines. However, while women and men lead differently, both approaches have their strengths, and neither is better than the other. As we have said, there is great value in combining the different approaches to leadership. When an organization effectively integrates women's and men's leadership styles, the result is a stronger, more nimble organization; it is an organization that is considered by employees as a good place to work.

You will be more successful if you lead in a woman's way. "Be authentic," advises Fiona O'Hara, Senior Executive, Technology Director of Operations at Accenture.[1]

What are women's strengths as leaders? How do you lead like a woman? In this chapter, we share with you the latest research on women's leadership styles and the strategies of women who have achieved the highest levels of success by maximizing their female strengths. Some of these strategies will resonate with you; others may not. The purpose of this chapter is to help you recognize and value the strengths that you, as a woman, bring to leadership and feel confident incorporating these strengths into your leadership style.

Women Are Learning to Lead Authentically

Women are holistic. When they look at their lives, they see the integration of family, professional, community, and personal goals and values rather than viewing each part of their life as a silo. They take into consideration people as whole individuals, with personal and professional goals and responsibilities. In business, women go beyond the specific situation to consider the relationship of other factors. While men focus primarily on facts, logic, and hierarchy, women add a context of values, vision, mission, and relationships. When women consider a situation, they see more than the facts on the table. They ask "why" as well as "what." As a result, they are likely to identify opportunities, risks, and gaps that men may not have recognized.

Camye Mackey, Vice President of Human Resources at the B. F. Saul Company Hospitality Group, sees this difference all the time. "Generally speaking, men tend to focus on the facts," says Camye. "Women are more likely to supplement the facts with a 360-degree view of the situation, looking at organizational and people implications that often are not reflected in the numbers."

Women's leadership strengths are characteristic of what is known as a transformational style of leadership, a style that is inclusive and consultative, and that generates employee commitment to the success of the organization. According to Bernard M. Bass, one of the leading management theorists, transformational leadership is imperative to success in today's global economy, and, he reports, women are more likely than men to embrace this style.[2]

This collaborative, consultative process results in better decisions and buy-in that can dramatically reduce the time it takes to implement change. Transformational leaders create a shared vision and shared ownership with employees in achieving that vision. They create an atmosphere that is intellectually stimulating, values-based, and respectful of individual differences.

Transformational leadership breaks with the more traditional style of transactional leadership, which is based on the carrot-and-stick approach to management. Transactional leaders motivate employees by appealing to their self-interest, establishing goals, and rewarding desired behaviors.

Women recognize the importance of rewards. However, women use rewards differently from transactional leaders. Rather than using rewards as motivators, women use shared goals to provide motivation and use individual rewards to recognize contributions to the organization's success.

Women Are Inclusive and Collaborative

Women value building relationships. They build strong, productive relationships with employees horizontally across the company with other functions and business areas, and outside the company with customers and vendors. These relationships become the foundation for inclusive and collaborative problem solving and decision making.

The best women leaders recognize that they cannot be experts in every area. Rather, they surround themselves with people who have greater expertise and skills than they do in given areas. They value diversity in backgrounds and perspectives because this gives the group wider expertise and flexibility. They are more inclusive when putting together teams or creating small groups to address specific situations. The result is more creative and nontraditional solutions. "The more senior you become, the more you know you can't be an expert in everything. But, you do know you can become a good synthesizer of information and use that to make good decisions based on the information from the people around you," says Judith (Judy) Robinson, Colonel, Medical Service Corps, United States Army.

Women shine in facilitating group dynamics. They are more likely to start by examining the problem and to consider, "are we asking the right questions" before moving to developing solutions. They encourage all group members to share their ideas and insights, ensure that everyone has the opportunity to speak, and focus on synthesizing all the ideas into a common solution that is stronger and more creative than the solution any one individual might have developed. A woman is not concerned with competing to have her personal solution to the problem accepted or getting the credit for the good idea; to her, the primary objective is to generate the best possible solution to a challenge.

Not surprisingly, when the Massachusetts Institute of Technology (MIT) undertook a study to determine what factors lead to successful group problem solving, they found the presence of women leaders was the critical component. Groups with women leaders surpassed all other groups in producing high-quality solutions, even when other groups had a higher average IQ or included one or two team members with extremely high IQs. What differentiated the most successful groups was having leaders who made certain that everyone had the opportunity to speak regardless of seniority or status, who listened, and who synthesized ideas to create a solution that integrated the best ideas of the entire group. When the researchers reviewed the composition of the top-performing groups, they found that these groups included women members.[3] The women's nonconfrontational styles created an environment in which group members felt safe in taking risks and putting forth their most creative and often nontraditional ideas. While men certainly can learn these skills, women excel at the nuances of motivating group members to share their expertise and combine their knowledge to create new solutions or beef up existing processes.

This style of collaborative decision making is the wave of the future in business, and men are as aware as women of its value. When Virginia Rometty was announced as IBM's new CEO, one of her former customers applauded the decision because he saw her skills at collaborative leadership as crucial to the future of the IT industry. He had become acquainted with Virginia Rometty when he was president and COO of Coca-Cola, and she was leading the IBM team working on Coca-Cola's information technology needs. "Under her direction, IBM staffers engaged in collaborative problem solving which I think the future of IT is all about."[4]

Women Invest Time in Consultation

Women take time to consult with others when making a decision. They pull together those who will be affected by the decision or who will have to implement the solution—employees, colleagues, customers, and vendors—to discuss the pros and cons of the decision. The result is both buy-in from those affected by the decision and improved decisions. Women truly want to know what others think about a decision. In talking with women leaders about what they do differently, a key factor is the consultative process. They say they ask for others' ideas and recommendations, and, most important, really listen to the responses and incorporate them into making the final decision. Women are more open to considering alternative solutions and more willing to compromise to achieve the overall objective.

One of the concerns some harbor about women leaders is that

they may take longer than men to make decisions. Women know when to be decisive. If a critical decision must be made quickly, women will not delay making it. When given their preference, however, they will invest the time to consult. In addition to generating better decisions, one of the advantages of women's consultative approach is that when the decision is made, the risks already have been addressed, and those who will implement the decision already are committed. The result is faster and often more effective implementation.

Women Create Shared Vision, Shared Values, and Shared Goals

Women place a high level of importance on values and vision. They place great weight on the values and vision of the company when choosing a place to work, and the values and vision are a major factor in why they choose to stay with a company. This focus on values and vision carries over into the way they lead. Women take time to articulate and generate employee commitment to their vision and organizational values. Shared vision and values translate into commitment to shared goals, which leads to organizational success.

Women want to understand how overall organizational goals contribute to business success and how the goals of their function tie into the overall organizational goals. Women make a priority of communicating to their employees what their business unit's goals are, how these goals contribute to the function's success, and how they tie into the overall business. As a result, they engender employee engagement and commitment to achieving the vision and goals of the business unit and, therefore, the overall business.

Women Lead Holistically

Women's holistic perspective extends to employees. They realize employees do not park their personal goals and responsibilities at the door when they come to work. Women leaders get to know their employees and create an environment, in which achieving professional goals for the company results in employees also achieving their personal aspirations and goals. Research shows that as a result of this leadership style, employees report a higher level of trust in women leaders than in men leaders and believe women leaders are more likely to understand what employees face in their personal lives. When employees feel this way, they become more committed to the goals of the organization and will invest the effort and time to go the extra mile to achieve the goals.

Both men and women employees are more likely to say they trust a woman leader than a man leader, according to a recent survey of a broad spectrum of global companies. Male and female employees in companies headed by a woman CEO expressed a higher level of trust in their CEO than employees in companies headed by male CEOs. And when times get tough, the difference in level of trust increases. A follow-up survey found that as the recent recession hit Europe, the male employees' level of trust in their female CEO went up significantly, while levels of trust in male CEOs remained constant.

Employees also reported a higher level of confidence that their woman CEO knows what she is doing. In the same survey, employees ranked women CEOs higher than their men counterparts in their ability to do the job and on being principled and honest, reflecting women's focus on shared values and vision.[5]

Results like these should add to women's confidence in leading in their own style. They show how far we have come in valuing the unique skills women bring to leadership. Styles that once were dismissed as inappropriate in business leadership now are valued as integral to generating employee commitment and performance.

This level of trust in their leader is what motivates employees to become members of high-performing teams that achieve goals and contribute to the success of the company. This is perhaps women's greatest strength—their ability to command the highest levels of commitment from others to achieve the organization's mission and vision.

An excellent example of the impact of women's leadership strengths is the story of high school football coach Natalie Randolph. She demonstrates women's ability to command the highest levels of commitment from their teams and to inspire them to achieve a goal none of the team members would have believed possible. In Natalie's case, the achievement was playing in the annual Turkey Bowl, the most prestigious public school sports event in Washington, D.C. In the previous quarter of a century, the high school where she coached had made it to the Turkey Bowl only once.

Coach Randolph is probably the only woman in the country coaching high school football. When she arrived a year earlier, skepticism about her ability to coach a boys' football team had been rampant—in the school and in the press. "I had no other choice," says Natalie. "I had to succeed." The school's football program was in a shambles, and many of the team members regularly skipped classes and had no ambitions beyond playing high school football. Natalie made academics as important as football, focused the team members on their future beyond simply graduating from high school, and created a strong team culture. Today, her players are no longer skeptical, and they want to play for her. "We trust her," says one of the seniors on the team. "She focuses on our futures, not just football. It makes me feel great that we can do this for her and for ourselves, to take the first lady to the Turkey Bowl in her second year." As the players prepared for their first Turkey Bowl, they told a newspaper reporter, "We're going all out for Ms. Randolph and for our high school." While the team did not win the game, the players won respect for themselves, for the team, and for the school. It was a win for the boys, but most of all, it was a win for Natalie Randolph—no longer is anyone questioning whether a woman can coach boys' football.[6]

Women Can Be Both Collaborative and Decisive

The perennial question is: can a woman be collaborative, inclusive, and consultative and still make the tough decisions? When Time Inc. selected Laura Lang as its new CEO, her former boss, a man, praised her as being "all about the team." "I've always been inclusive and collaborative," said Ms. Lang in an interview. "I also know how to make decisions. One does not preclude the other."[7]

Women know when and how to make the tough decisions and

do not shirk this responsibility. The challenge is communicating the tough decisions. While men have the same challenge when faced with communicating a tough decision, the challenge is greater for women because they are expected to be compassionate and caring. When they do not behave that way, their behavior is interpreted more severely than a man's would be. One of women's strengths is their ability to communicate tough decisions while at the same time letting people know that they are respected and are being treated fairly. They acknowledge that they are aware of how the decision will affect each person and provide assurance that these factors have been considered in the decision-making process.

As a result of the recent recession, Susan Helstab, Executive Vice President of Marketing at Four Seasons Hotels and Resorts, had to make the decision to lay off salespeople for the first time in the history of the company. "It was like the sales offices were struck by lightning because they never believed anything like this could be possible," says Susan. She acted based on wisdom she had gained from the company's founder: "What people are going to remember is not what you did, but how you did it." She says she worked to deliver the bad news in such a way that people would feel they had been treated fairly and with respect, and would want to work for the company again.

Women's concern for people and relationships helps them deliver tough messages in a way that communicates their concern for the individual. They present the decision in terms of the needs of the business rather than the individual's worth as a human being. Even when firing an employee, the action often can be presented as a lack of a match between the individual's skills and the company's needs rather than focusing on the employee's failure to perform.

Delivering bad news is not limited to talking to employees. Sometimes customers or vendors have to be told something they will not like. Men often ask a woman to come along when the news is bad. This is where the power of women's relationship building makes a real difference. As with employees, the key, say successful businesswomen, is treating everyone with respect and always being honest. When there is an existing relationship of trust, it is easier to deliver bad news in a way that preserves the relationship, feels fair, and minimizes negative feelings.

Women Are Skilled at Multitasking

Multitasking is one of the strengths men often ascribe more to women than to themselves. Women attribute their skill at multitasking to the multiple demands they face every day as a professional, a wife, a mother, a daughter, and manager of the household affairs. This skill not only helps them manage their time more effectively, but helps them be more effective in dealing with unexpected emergencies at work or in other parts of their lives. While men leaders view unscheduled visits by staff or peers as interruptions, women leaders tend to welcome them as a way of keeping their finger on the pulse of the organization.[8]

Judy Robinson focuses on multitasking as one of the core strengths women bring to leadership. "Growing up on a farm, I learned that you could never do just one job—you were juggling several, while thinking about others, getting them all organized in your brain," says Judy. "Whether it was planting, butchering, preserving, cooking, or a plethora of others, I learned to weave it all together, and to think about the myriad of little details that move you from good to as close to perfection as possible. My day in the Army may be in a different environment, but it is still that collection of tasks with a myriad of details to track."

Weaving the priorities together makes women more effective as leaders, helps them integrate their professional and personal lives, and adds to their contribution to the success of the business.

Realize Women's Leadership Styles Have a Foundation in Science

Women's leadership strengths are not happenstance. Neuroscience, the science of the brain, provides insight into the differences between women's and men's leadership styles. As neuroscience has become more sophisticated, researchers are able to observe and track brain activity using a variety of imaging technologies that identify which areas of the brain are active while performing different tasks such as problem solving, meetings, negotiations, and other activities. Comparing activity in women's and men's brains when reacting to business situations, researchers consistently found what we all knew intuitively—women's and men's brain activity is different.[9]

What is interesting and important is that brain activity differences affect the path women and men take to problem solving, but not the quality of the outcome. Women and men are equally effective in achieving goals, regardless of the differences in the way they approach problems.[10]

Women's brains show activity in more areas distributed across the brain than men's brains when engaged in tasks such as problem-solving situations. This helps explain the holistic and integrative view women bring to business and their propensity to multitask. Multiple brain studies looking at problem-solving activities show that men are likely to use only one area of the brain, while women use multiple areas of the brain. Using a broader network of different brain regions also leads to greater creativity and a wider array of possible solutions. The difference is likely due to the proportion of white and gray matter in male and female brains. Women have proportionately more white matter, which supports connections across areas of the brain. Men have proportionately more gray matter, which focuses brain activity into a single region of the brain.[11] The result is that women are continuously making connections among facts and relationships as part of problem solving, which accounts for their more holistic perspective when viewing and solving problems.

Researchers also report that scans show that women display more neural activity in the parts of the brain supporting the use of language and in the connections in the brain affecting memories, emotions, and sensory clues. As a result, women are more likely than men to consider relationships and values while simultaneously focusing on facts and logic. These findings also support results in other research showing women's preference for talking through decisions and discussing relationships.

Differences in brain chemistry also play a role in the difference between how women and men approach leadership. Women's brains secrete higher levels of two chemicals, serotonin and oxytocin. Serotonin regulates moods and calms our impulses. Oxytocin is believed to be involved in social bonding and creates a substantial increase in trust among humans. This is one reason women give high priority to creating a culture of trust with their employees and building relationships.

The differences in brain chemistry also affect the way women and men deal with conflict. Women have lower levels of testosterone and vasopressin than men; these are chemicals that encourage aggression and territoriality. The structure in the brain that is associated with aggressive action, fear, and anxiety (the amygdala) is smaller in women. When women get angry or threatened, they are less likely to react with aggressive action and more likely to focus on understanding the emotional and interpersonal aspects of the situation. As a consequence, women's leadership style is more likely than men's to include listening and compromise.[12]

The research does not imply that the differences between women and men are "hard-wired" into the brain. In fact, the latest research shows that the brain is remarkably plastic. The strength of brain activity can be changed by practicing specific activities. So men can become more adept at the skills that make women effective, and women can become more adept at the skills that make men effective.[13] Many women and men are already broadening their leadership styles to include practices we have traditionally characterized as male or female. The differences in leadership perspectives are not in conflict; they are complementary. Since research shows each of these leadership styles leads to effective solutions, think how much more effective every enterprise could be if it tapped into the full value of women's leadership strengths and integrated them with men's leadership strengths. The most successful leaders are creating organizations that value and encourage this integrative approach to leadership.

Lead Like a Woman

Successful women are true to themselves. They act authentically and complement their business acumen with their female leadership strengths. It is neither necessary nor advisable to behave like one of the boys.

Kathleen (Kate) Nealon, Non-executive Director at Argo Group International Holdings, Ltd. and retired Group Head of Legal and Compliance at Standard Chartered Plc., says she spent too many years worrying about trying to fit into a mold she would never fit into. "Embrace the differences," says Kate. "I was never going to be one of the guys. They know you are not the same, and you know you are not the same when you are being realistic."

Josette Sherman, Executive Director of the World Food Program, told the *Washington Post*, "There was a point in my career when I thought, 'If I don't curse a lot when I'm talking to people, maybe I'm not a leader.' Because, it's what I knew." She continued, "For women, I think the toughest thing is figuring out how to assert their authority in a way that's true to themselves."[14]

People like women to behave like women. If you act contrary to expectations of women as leaders, it creates dissonance, and dissonance makes people uncomfortable. However, the value of leading in a relational style goes well beyond avoiding dissonance. Women's leadership style makes others feel valued, committed to achieving organizational goals, and appreciated. Being true to your women's leadership preferences in no way precludes establishing demanding goals, asking the tough questions, making the hard decisions, and addressing performance problems. The value of your woman's leadership style is how you handle the tough issues, a way that is appreciated by your employees and managers. Fiona O'Hara, Senior Executive, Technology Director of Operations at Accenture, says one of the things she wishes she had known earlier is that "it's as much about how you do things as what you do or know."[15]

"Don't stop being a woman just because you are in a job," adds

Judy Robinson. She says she has seen some women in the Army who try to be more male than the men. "You don't have to give up being a woman just to be in a man's world."

Sometimes it is the little things that make a big difference in the atmosphere and culture of the office. Women are likely to bring a plant or flowers for the reception area, celebrate birthdays, or take the time to inquire about a sick child. People appreciate these simple actions. It is part of what makes them feel valued as team members.

"It is important to women leaders to stay true to themselves. Don't change your behavior because you think it is too much like a woman," says Judy Robinson. "When I brought a plant into the waiting area at a battalion aid station, I got a lot of ribbing about how 'girly' that was. But when some young infantry guys commented on how great it was to see something like this—and expected plants to continue showing up, I knew I had done the right thing."

Position Yourself for the Future

Women's leadership styles are the style of the future. Globalization is forcing businesses to solve problems differently, deal with increasing national cultural diversity, respond to unprecedented and unpredictable change, and energize a workforce whose values and work ethics are dramatically different from those of the past. The way we work has changed as well. Technology has led to virtual teams with members located around the world. Ethical issues are becoming more complex. Around the globe, businesses, governments, and nongovernmental organizations (NGOs) all are confronting the same challenges.

Women's leadership strengths are the very skills that management theorists, consultants, and corporate leaders say are critical in the new global economy. Effective leadership in a global world will empower diverse, geographically dispersed groups of people to work together toward a common vision and common goals.[16] This will require leaders who value diversity and are visionary, are open to new ideas and ways of doing work, are collaborative, and are team builders.

Future success is not based on doing what worked in the past. It is about creating new values, new ways of doing business, and new ways of collaborating to achieve common goals. It is about seeing the world through a different lens. Successful women say that one of their advantages is not being bound by the "way it has always been done." When women become leaders, they create what they see as the best way to do the job—which often is a new approach—and one that works.

Empower the Woman Leader Within:
In Summary

- Become confident leading like a woman.
- Lead authentically.
  - Be inclusive and collaborative.
  - Invest time in consultation.
  - Create shared vision, shared values, and shared goals.
  - Lead holistically.
  - Be collaborative and be tough.
  - Value women's ability to multitask.
  - Realize women's leadership styles have a foundation in science.
- Lead like a woman.
- Prepare for the future: women's leadership styles are the style of the future.

Own Your Destiny

True success is how you define it for yourself. All too often, women's definition of success is based on what they believe others expect of them. Free yourself up to define success based on your own values, passions, and vision. Success Strategy Two provides the insight to recognize and break free of the boundaries you were not aware were influencing you and holding you back from achieving all that you have the potential to be and creating your personal vision for your life.

Break Free of the Boundaries

When you think about your future, do you limit yourself from reaching for the highest levels? Do you dream really big dreams but dismiss them as being unrealistic? When you dismiss goals as being unrealistic, you very likely are responding, without even realizing it, to cultural or family expectations for women.

We know from the studies of women's leadership that one of women's strengths is their sensitivity to others' thoughts and feelings. This is what makes women excel at group dynamics and relationship building. On the downside, women are extremely sensitive to others' expectations about the role of women. The problem is that, without realizing it, this awareness influences women to conform to cultural definitions of acceptable behavior and goals for women and the expectations of friends and family.

These expectations often result in self-limitations, which undermine women's self-confidence and lead them to doubt their own potential. They influence the way women behave, the goals women establish, the risks women take, and the way women define success. When women do break with tradition and take on roles that are inconsistent with cultural, organizational, or family expectations, they often feel guilty and start rationalizing their choices to themselves and to others.

These stereotypes become barriers to owning your own destiny and having the confidence to develop and pursue your personal goals. They lead you to act as others would have you act, rather than following your dreams and acting on your instincts.

Identify the Boundaries Holding You Back

You must recognize where your personal boundaries originate and examine the pressures arising from others' expectations. Understand how these stereotypes are affecting your goals, perception of self-worth, belief in your capabilities and potential, and the way you behave. This is more difficult than it seems because you often are unaware that you are, in fact, adjusting your behavior in response to others' stereotypes.

Boundaries often are created by those who care about you the most and whom you respect and want to make happy. Your parents, relatives, husbands or partners, friends, and even your children have expectations about what constitutes success for a woman—marriage, children, a clean house, being a good cook, actively volunteering for your children's school or your community—and the list goes on. Even today, having a flourishing career often is not part of other people's definitions of success for you. Families expect men to become presidents of their companies or of the nation; they expect women to have a "little" career or start a small, hobby business.

As more women move into the workforce, these stereotypes are changing. Both boys and girls see their mothers happily and successfully pursuing careers. Sharon's mother had four children, had a successful marriage, and was an award-winning chemistry professor. In addition, she pioneered models for teaching science to children with physical and learning disabilities. Her goal for her three daughters was for them to become economically independent. "I want my girls to always be able to earn enough to support themselves no matter what happens," she told her daughters repeatedly.

How are you affected by the expectations of those you love and respect the most? Hopefully, they are opening up the world for you. If not, create a new scenario for yourself that fits your aspirations.

As women move from the family to the professional environment, they confront different, but equally powerful, expectations that create boundaries. They are expected to adopt the prevailing definition of business success—working long hours, being available 24/7, traveling at the drop of a hat, and valuing being rewarded with a corner office—where they are expected to be even more available, do even more travel, and work even longer hours.

Yet women's goals often are different. While they want to be recognized through promotions and increased responsibility, they believe successful completion of projects and tasks is the most important. The move toward more flexible workplaces is starting to put a small, but important, crack in the traditional definition of corporate success.

Workplace expectations go beyond the reward structure. Cultural stereotypes that women will not take risks, are too "soft" to make the tough decisions, and are not right for certain jobs not only influence what men expect of women in the workplace, they also still influence how women behave. What is especially pernicious about these expectations is they usually are unspoken and often unconscious. So recognizing the impact of these workplace expectations and breaking through them is surprisingly challenging.

A dramatic study opens our eyes to the dramatic impact these expectations can have on the way women behave starting at an early age. This study compares high school girls' performance in selecting high-risk/high-reward options when in single gender groups and in mixed gender groups. In the single gender groups, the girls took high risks to maximize rewards; in the mixed gender groups, the girls selected the lower-risk options despite the reduction in rewards.

The important finding in this study is not about risk—although that is interesting. The significance of this study is how girls' behavior changed unconsciously in the presence of boys. Two societal gender stereotypes influence these results:

- The expectations of males that women should not be risk takers.
- The belief by females that males believe it is inappropriate for women to aspire to maximizing rewards.

Without consciously making a decision to take less risk and forgo rewards, when the girls were in mixed groups, they nevertheless acted consistent with boys' stereotypes about appropriate behavior for women. In contrast, the boys' performance did not vary based on the group's gender composition. Gender stereotypes for men include taking high risks and maximizing rewards.[1] The researchers speculate that this *unconscious* adapting to men's stereotypes of women contributes to women's reluctance to negotiate for higher salaries or advocate for themselves with senior management who are mostly men.

Take Action

How do you break free of these boundaries, especially the ones you are not consciously aware of, and achieve your full potential? Highly accomplished women say that believing in themselves and their ability to take control and develop their destiny are what make them successful. These women are confident in their capabilities, trust their instincts, and establish extraordinarily high goals. They have the courage to take a leap of faith, define success on their own terms, and create their own path. They have become skilled at integrating their business skills and their women's leadership strengths to maximize their success in all aspects of their lives.

Believe in Yourself

Self-confidence, however, does not always come early or easily. In a recent survey of members of the Committee of 200, an organization of women leaders at the highest echelons of business, when asked what they wished they had known earlier in their careers, respondents said, "To trust my instincts and move forward in my own way."[2]

Learning to trust your instincts and acknowledge your strengths is the foundation for developing self-confidence. Women are more likely than men to question their capabilities. Men tend to overinflate their actual capabilities and blame external circumstances when they are not successful. Women rank their capabilities more modestly, often understating them, and respond to not being successful by turning inward to examine themselves.[3] They are likely to internalize failure and question whether they have the ability to do the job. Even when things are going well, women may have that niggling sense of self-doubt that tells them they are faking it and everyone will soon recognize that.

"I had to learn to trust my judgment and recognize that I am responsible for creating my own success," wrote one respondent to the Committee of 200 survey. Recognizing this is a key turning point for most women in their careers.

Successful women have confidence in themselves and in their capacity to solve problems. Self-confidence goes beyond believing you have a specific skill or talent. Self-confidence involves believing in your ability to coordinate and orchestrate your skills to conquer a challenging situation. Confident women see themselves controlling and managing their environment. When things go wrong, they look to diagnose what is happening in the environment, not just themselves; they look to change the environment, not themselves. They analyze the situation, search for trends or discontinuities, look at the facts, and identify possible solutions.

Laura calls this ability to analyze the situation and develop solutions "Figure It Out Smarts." Successful women are comfortable facing the unknown, believing they know how to figure out what is required to be successful. They are confident in their ability to learn and secure enough to ask for help when they need it.

The core of "Figure It Out Smarts" is a proven set of skills and traits that enable women to "figure out" how they can do it. It combines their belief in themselves, their direct experiences, and the knowledge they gain through research and from experts in the field who have related experience. Women with these traits build on their strength of pulling together people with the experience and expertise to understand the situation and the creativity to contribute to developing new solutions.

Take Charge of Your Success

A significant part of self-confidence is recognizing that you, not others, are in charge of your success and can establish any goals you wish. You believe you can accomplish anything you set out to do because you are confident in yourself and in the value of your goals.[4] Beverly Holmes, Founder and CEO, B. A. Holmes & Associates; Retired, Senior Vice President, Retirement Services Division at MassMutual Financial Group, says her success is the result of "my focus and faith—faith in God, faith in my ability to overcome obstacles, and the tenacity to stay totally focused on my desired outcome."

Confident women believe in their goals and take ownership of creating the situations needed to achieve them. Kim Roberts, Director of Government Analysis at Science Applications International Corporation (SAIC), says, "I feel that what I've done, I've done personally. While I had the support of the company, I didn't succeed because of the company. I succeeded because of myself. When I decided I would get an interview with Yasser Arafat when he was in Tunisia, it wasn't the company that put things in motion. I did it through personal relationships. I've had to be pretty scrappy, and I'm proud of that."

Be Comfortable Being Uncomfortable

Successful women are comfortable being uncomfortable. Men will snap up an opportunity to assume new responsibilities or a high-profile position regardless of whether they have related experience. Women are likely to demur, concerned that they don't have the experience to do the job successfully.

Virginia Rometty, CEO of IBM, speaking at *Fortune*'s "Most Powerful Women" Conference, recounted a time when she was offered a new position. She asked for time to think about it, and that night, talking with her husband, she declared she needed more time to develop the experience and skills required for the job. He asked if she thought that was what a man would say. The next day, she accepted the position. She told the audience that she had learned throughout her career to always take jobs that put you in a zone you don't know, that "Comfort and growth cannot coexist."

Successful women have the confidence they will rise to any challenges they take on. "Don't shy away from challenges and stretch roles," advises Fiona O'Hara, Senior Executive, Technology Director of Operations at Accenture. She says you learn more by taking on challenges than by staying in your comfort zone. "It can also provide an opportunity to show what you are capable of and in doing so serve to advance your career more quickly."[5]

At *Fortune*'s "Most Powerful Women" Conference, Meg Whitman, CEO of Hewlett-Packard (HP), was asked what accounted for her willingness to take on high-profile challenges. "I have this courage gene," responded Ms. Whitman. All highly successful women seem to have this courage gene that propels them to seek out new and challenging opportunities, take a stand for what they believe in, and transform traditional ways of operating in business and in their personal lives. When you are courageous, you can change the world.

Be Resilient and Persistent

Women have amazing resilience. They develop backup plans for every contingency, in both their business and their personal lives. They bounce back from disappointments or failures, applying what they learned to the next opportunity. Meg Whitman spent two and a half years running for governor of California and lost. She reports she licked her wounds for about six months. Then she told herself to pull up her socks and get back out there. She joined the HP board of directors and, in fall 2011, when the company was in financial and strategic distress, she agreed to take over as CEO to deal with the crisis. In the interview at *Fortune*'s "Most Powerful Women" Conference, she said it was the experiences she had while running for governor that gave her the confidence to take on the challenges of leading HP in its time of turmoil.

Self-confident women are persistent. If one approach does not work, they develop another way to achieve the goal. In pursuit of an important goal, they have the courage to continue forward no matter the odds. Nina McLemore, Founder and CEO, Nina McLemore, LLC, former Founder and President of Liz Claiborne Accessories, and member of the executive committee of Liz Claiborne Inc., says, "What I learned from climbing Mount Kilimanjaro is that you can get through anything if you just breathe deeply and keep putting one foot in front of the other."

Kim Roberts says perseverance has played a crucial role in her success. "I feel really proud of persevering," says Kim, "because some of the things I have done are terrifying. I don't mean in a physical sense; I mean having no clue what I was doing, and yet I was successful." Her first job was at United Press International (UPI) taking dictation, but she did not know how to type. "Reporters like Helen Thomas would call in, and I would have the phone tucked between my shoulder and my ear and they would start dictating their stories. So I would type a couple of letters from each word, go to the bathroom and hyperventilate, and then go back and fill out the words as I recalled them. I was terrified. It was horrible to have to do something you don't know how to do. I always look back on that, saying if I could get through that, I can get through anything. You have to shake yourself up and make that first step, even though it is terrifying." By the time she left the job at UPI, she had become one of the fastest dictationists they ever had.

Benefit from Failure: Learn, Laugh, and Move On
Self-confident women take risks knowing they will not always be successful. Mistakes happen. Projects fail. When confronted with obstacles, women who believe in themselves focus on diagnosing

their tasks and taking action, while those who do not are likely to turn inward and focus on their own inadequacies.

For years, women have been overachievers. They feared, often with reason, that when they made even a single mistake, it would be blown out of proportion as proof that they were not capable of doing the job. However, striving for perfection is unrealistic. It prevents you from taking risks and trying new ways to accomplish goals. More important than never making a mistake is figuring out how to fix the mistake and what actions to take to prevent it from happening again.

A thought-provoking article, "The Failure Imperative," suggests that learning to deal with failure is crucial in today's fast-changing, technology-based business environment.[6] Successful leaders must take high risks to stay ahead of the competition and be willing to both succeed and fail spectacularly. Separate your personal competencies and sense of self from the failure or the mistake. You as an individual are not inadequate or incompetent.

Do not wallow in failure. View failure as an opportunity to learn—either what not to do in the future or how to make necessary corrections. Review the situation and see what you could have done differently. Identify what you can learn from the failure and how you can apply that in the future. If others were involved, bring them together to do a postmortem of what went wrong and what went well. Teach others how to benefit from failure rather than lose confidence in themselves. Mary Cantando, a growth expert for the Woman's Advantage, has a client who greets every failure or mistake with the words "how fascinating." The client then goes on to figure out how she would handle the situation in the future and if action is needed in the present.[7] Make failures fascinating learning experiences.

Most successful businesswomen say they do not regret their failures and, if they could change their careers, they would not change the failures. Your failures are part of your ultimate success. Angela Ahrendts, CEO of Burberry, was number eight on the *Financial Times'* list of "The Top 50 Women in World Business, 2011." In her profile, she says she has few regrets. "She can point to unsuccessful phases of her career, 'but when I look back on what I learned . . . I don't think there's anything I'd change because if I did, I may not have had the honor to be in the position I'm in today.'"[8]

Follow the lead of the most successful women when you fail— learn from your experience, as soon as possible, laugh about the mistake, and then move on. Kim Roberts puts it this way, "There are things that haven't turned out perfectly, but in the big picture, I don't have a lot of regrets. Everybody has a fear of failure, but I've been humiliated enough in my life I know how to handle it. I laugh—you have to have a sense of humor."

Set High Goals to Drive Success

The value of high goals is not just a motivational myth! High goals result in high levels of accomplishment. In fact, the only statistically significant predictor of whether a woman will obtain expansion capital for her business and ultimately grow it is not her industry, the size of her business, or the length of her time in business. It is her goal for growth. The higher the goal, the more likely she is to obtain the capital she needs.[9]

Confident women establish challenging goals and believe they can achieve them. Setting high goals becomes a self-fulfilling prophecy. How many times have you heard the phrase, "If you think you can, you can; if you think you can't, you can't"? Research and experience prove the truth of this statement.

Take for example, Sandra Cauffman. She is living her dream. She is an engineer by training and currently project manager for the Gravity and Extreme Magnetism Small Explorer Phase A Study at the National Aeronautics and Space Administration (NASA). Take it from those at the Goddard Space Flight Center who know, this is an impressive position. Sandra says, "Working for NASA was my childhood dream. I was born in Costa Rica, and coming to the United States was not even a possibility. But dreams may come true when you put your mind to them and continually do your best. At the very least, aiming high allows you to get that much farther than the alternative. It is an honor to be part of the NASA family."[10]

Establishing ambitious professional goals early is important because your goals influence the way you act. If your goal is to be a first-line supervisor, you will act like a first-line supervisor; if your goal is to be a divisional president, you will act like a potential divisional president. You behave differently, present yourself differently, and make decisions differently when your goal is to be a member of senior management. Your goals influence the positions you seek, the educational opportunities you undertake, and the way you network. The relationships and networks you build, the mentors you seek, and the sponsors you develop reflect your goals. Having high goals influences the path you will follow and drives you to set interim goals that increase your readiness for leadership growth. Your actions create an image of you as a leader in the minds of senior management, your peers, and your employees. High goals create a self-fulfilling prophecy.

Setting high goals keeps your options open. At the beginning of your career, you may not be certain of your direction. By establishing high goals from the start, you will do what is necessary to develop the foundation of education, experience, and networks required to achieve highly ambitious professional goals. If after three to five years, you decide to pursue other goals, you can. You will have gained useful experience. If, however, you do indeed want to go for the gold ring in the corporate world, you will be positioned to move forward.

Establish goals that are important to you. You have to want to achieve something so much that you will never give up. Figure out what your passion is and what you believe is worth striving to achieve. Set your aspirations high and go for them. Dream big dreams, set high goals, and when you succeed, set even higher goals. Marilyn Johnson, Retired Vice President of Market Development at IBM, says, "Every time I achieved my dreams—getting hired, becoming a manager, or even getting the VP title, I asked myself what I could do next. How can I dream even bigger and turn that into reality? Your dreams can become your life."

Marilyn continues, "If young women are watching me, I hope they look beyond what I have achieved, and know they can be CEOs.

You have to think about your goals." The most successful women in business set extremely high goals for themselves, and when they achieve those goals, they ratchet them up even higher.

Own Your Success

One of women's strengths is recognizing and rewarding other people's contributions. Women enjoy shining the spotlight on others, and, indeed, one of their strengths is recognizing and rewarding performance. However, they often showcase others and take a backseat for themselves because they believe they should not be the center of attention or grab credit. When complimented, women often brush off the praise by saying, "It wasn't me, it was the team," or "I had such great colleagues working with me." "Never apologize for your success," says Usha Pillai, Founder and President of Aria Management Consulting, LLC, and former Senior Director at Pfizer. "It is you who led that team, you who led your peers."

This was brought home to her when a senior executive complimented her on an accomplishment, and she brushed it off as being the team effort. Later, the executive told Usha that her reaction denigrated the compliment. "You are saying that I don't know what I am talking about when I compliment you for doing a good job," she said. "Learn to be gracious and say thank you when complimented and take pride that your accomplishment has been acknowledged."

"We love to give credit to other people because that's the way women are," says Kathe Albrecht, Visual Resources Curator at American University. "I think we work better in groups. But we don't take credit when the great idea is ours. Men would just say they did it. But women, because we are looking at 360 degrees and the people relationships, tend not take the credit because we want the group effect. But I think it is very important to give yourself credit when it's due."

Others—your manager, senior executives, or your employees—will see you as a model of success and a candidate for leadership only if you present yourself that way. If you keep giving away the credit, your employees or colleagues will begin to believe that indeed they are the ones who have made the business or the project successful and that you were superfluous. In addition to detracting from your image as an effective leader, this often creates overly ambitious expectations for compensation and organizational rewards.

When Laura sold her company, she was surprised at the number of senior officers who approached her to ask for a larger piece of the sales price. Their rationale was that they had really been more important to the success of the business than she. When asked if they had done the activities involved in building a company—managing all the contracts, serving as technical monitor, investing their savings, going without a salary, or putting their home up as collateral for the loans to finance the company—they began to understand what building a company really means. Laura recognized that by not taking credit for all she had done and sharing the demands and risks required to build a company, her senior staff minimized her contributions.

"Don't give away the credit to the team by discounting your own contribution," says Usha Pillai. "It doesn't mean the team wasn't important; it just means you had a significant role in the team's success. Accept that."

Take ownership of your success. Give credit where credit is due, but make certain your colleagues, employees, and senior management recognize your role and your accomplishments.

Break Free of the Boundaries: In Summary

- Identify the boundaries that are holding you back.
- Take action.
  - Believe in yourself.
  - Take charge of your success.
  - Be comfortable being uncomfortable.
  - Be resilient and persistent.
  - Benefit from failure: learn, laugh, and move on.

- Set high goals to drive success.
- Own your success.

Define Success in Your Own Terms

Only you can define what success means to you. Define success in terms of what is most fulfilling to you. Highly successful women say doing it their own way rather than striving to achieve what other people define as success is the only path to having a fulfilling and satisfying life. Living your definition of success makes life exciting and overcoming the challenges worthwhile.

Your definition of success affects every decision you make and every goal you establish in all aspects of your life. It is a critical process. Your personal definition of success takes into account all you want to achieve over a lifetime. It gives you the context for making both the long-term and the day-to-day decisions about all facets of your life. It will help you see your path clearly, set priorities, and accomplish your goals.

Women's definitions of success are holistic and multifaceted. The most successful women have developed an overall strategy to integrate all aspects of their lives: professional, family, community, and personal.[11] They have thought about and defined what they want to accomplish in their lives and what they want to achieve in all the different roles they play. They integrate their multiple roles thus achieving a holistic approach to life.

Think of this as your life strategy—the plan that defines what you will do to achieve your overarching purpose in life. It reflects your values and passions and incorporates your goals for every part of your life. It is flexible, and it can expand and change as your experiences and life change. Whether you are well into your career or just starting out, thinking strategically about yourself—how you define success and how you will achieve success—is energizing and meaningful.

Some women adopt a formal process and put their strategy in writing; others are more informal. All have searched their minds and hearts and developed an overall vision of how they want to live their lives and what they want to accomplish. Whatever approach you adopt, the critical thing is to thoughtfully and consciously develop your personal definition of success.

Defining success begins with knowing yourself—your values, passions, and strengths.

Know Yourself

Define Your Values and Live By Them
Values are your foundation for defining success and developing your life strategy. Define and embrace your values. Your values should apply to every aspect of your life. You cannot have one set of values at work and another set in your family life. Values are at the core of who you are and how you live your life. Everything else around you may be in flux and changing—but your values must remain rock solid at all times. In the Committee of 200's survey, "being clear about my values and following them consistently" ranks as one of the women's top five career accomplishments.

"In the end, you have to live with yourself," says Kim Roberts. "You can't be naïve, but you have to find your own personal line that you don't want to cross."

Your values are the lens through which you view every decision and determine the right action to take. According to Camye Mackey, "Knowing your values and holding true to them is critical when you run across situations in life or in the world of business that are new or difficult. You should allow your core beliefs and values to become your guiding principles in making solid decisions. You need to ask yourself if this is the right thing to do, and you need to make a commitment that a decision will not be made just because the solution might be more cost-effective."

The most successful businesswomen say they have the courage to act upon their values at all times in their personal and business lives. Moral courage is about applying your values consistently in everyday decisions, not just when confronted with the big choices. There is no such thing as a decision or an action so small that you can say, "It's okay to disregard my values—this is such a minor action." Even if no one else knows, you know, and ignoring your values makes you question yourself.

Maria Coyne, Executive Vice President, Head of the Consumer and Small Business Division at KeyBank, and member of the KeyCorp Executive Council, characterizes values as your compass. Integrity comes from acting based on your values. "Without integrity," says Maria, "you really have nothing. You are only as good as your name and the legacy of your actions, not just what you say. It is about how you act and the way you make people feel."

Some believe that "all is fair in love and in war," meaning that in business, it is not necessary to live by the values that drive your decisions in other parts of your life. These people believe it is acceptable to be ruthless in business. The women we interviewed believe you must know your values, and you must live by them in every aspect of your life. Women tell us, "To be your best, you must be consistent in who you are regardless of the setting."

Become consciously aware of your values, what they are, and how you expect them to play out in your life. Be able to articulate and communicate them clearly so they set the tone for your personal and professional behavior and for your business team and your family.

Find Your Passions

Your passions are those areas that bring out your highest level of excitement, motivation, and energy. Your passions define who you are. When you are passionate about something, you invest in the cause with your personal energy, imagination, time, and, when possible, money. While it is somewhat hard to define passion, it is not hard to recognize. Your entire body language changes when you speak about your passion. Others can see the passion in your eyes, hear it in your voice, and see it in the way you move.

"Love what you do," says Susan Helstab. "It makes a huge difference because work takes a lot of your time and it takes you away from other aspects of your life that are important to you, so it has to be worth it. It's not about the money. It is the satisfactions, growth opportunities, the ability to contribute to something you think is meaningful, and being with people you admire, respect, and like."

Passion is not a something that is fulfilled by a one-time goal or action. Pursuing your passion requires that you think in terms of a journey, not a specific objective. Being passionate is important to you as a leader. Your passion generates enthusiasm and energy in the people who work for you and with you. It makes them want to join you on your journey.

As you think about your goals in all areas of your life, take into account your values and passions. In particular, consider your professional life. Working in fields related to your passions will ensure that your job is exciting, rewarding, and fun. It will bring great job satisfaction and add meaning to your work life.

When Nancy Carosso, Physicist and Aerospace Engineer at the NASA Space Center, speaks about her career, you can feel her passion. "Working at NASA has truly been a gift. When you can say that you've never had a boring day at work—after thirty years—you truly are a lucky soul. Every mission, every day offers a new opportunity and a chance to learn. And then, through the mentoring programs, you have a chance to give back."[12]

Inventory Your Strengths and Weaknesses

Nina McLemore says to be successful in business, you must know and be realistic about your strengths and weaknesses. Take a hard look at yourself and be honest with yourself. This is not a time to be self-deprecating. Do not limit the list of strengths to what you see in your professional life. Think about what you do in your community and family life. Many times you use strengths in these arenas that you are not currently using in your professional life, but that may be transferable.

Take advantage of all your resources to help identify your strengths and weaknesses. Talk to coworkers about how they see you. Consult people you work with in your community and your professional associations. Ask your mentor or your manager what you should aspire to achieve. Mine what you can learn from performance reviews you have received.

Think about the times you are the most excited about what you are doing. Reflect on those moments when you truly see yourself as fantastic at your job or in volunteer activities. Consider what parts of your job are the most fulfilling, and worth any effort you have to invest. Work that is fun and feels easy usually builds on your strengths and passions. If you find the times you enjoy most are volunteer activities rather than at work, consider how you can move into a field consistent with your passions and strengths.

Consider what unique combinations of strengths you have. Include "soft" skills such as relationship building, team building, sales, and marketing as well as technical expertise such as information technology, engineering, or merchandising. The soft skills are especially important because as you move up in the business world, they begin to take precedence over your technical expertise as the key to performance and success.

Reflect on your weaknesses. Everyone has them! Learn to befriend them. No one is good at everything. It is as important to be aware of your weaknesses as your strengths. Avoid being overly self-critical. Accept that weaknesses are normal. What is important is to acknowledge your weaknesses and take the steps to compensate for them to avoid any negative impact. Unless it is vital for your career or personal life to become proficient in the area of a weakness, let it go. Far too many people invest substantial time and energy on proving they are good at what they do least well. Imagine how much more productive you would be if you focused the same amount of energy on what you do best.

This is not a one-time exercise. As you gain more experience, add to your education and training, advance in business, participate in community activities, and deal with family challenges, you will develop new insights and strengths. Take the time to evaluate and add to your list of strengths and weaknesses on a regular basis.

Define Success

Develop Your Guiding Vision

Your definition of success is based on what you want to achieve in life—what is important to you as an individual. Leadership guru Warren Bennis calls this your "guiding vision," and he says you cannot be a successful leader without discovering and owning your personal guiding vision.[13] This is your overarching purpose in life—your mission in life. It both reflects and is supported by your values and passions. It becomes the theme for all aspects of your life.

Women's guiding visions often incorporate making a difference for other people, for society, and for their organizations. Laura's guiding vision has always been to make the world a better place, and she did it by helping people get the information they needed to have better health. For Sharon, from her earliest days in business, it has been to provide women with the tools and knowledge to inspire them to achieve their full potential.

Monica Luechtefeld, Executive Vice President, E-Commerce and former member of the Executive Committee at Office Depot, says, "I want to be able to make a difference and leave something behind that is better for my having been there. That's what drives me personally, wanting to make a difference in the people and the projects that I touch."

Figure out what is right for you and keep it in view in everything you do.

Think Holistically

Break down your guiding vision and figure out its impact on every aspect of your life. The multiple aspects of your life are not silos surrounded by impermeable walls. Increasingly, both women and men recognize that the boundaries between the different parts of their life are permeable; that all aspects of their life complement and supplement each other. For example, you are likely to find your definition of professional success impacts your definition of success in your family life and vice versa.

As the women we interviewed looked back on their lives and identified the accomplishments they are most proud to have achieved, it was clear that their definition of success was the holistic integration of their goals in every aspect of their personal and professional lives. Both Beverly Holmes and Monica Luechtefeld are pioneers in their respective industries. Both led the development of highly successful new business areas for their companies that eventually influenced the direction of their respective industries. Both received many awards for their professional achievements and advanced to senior executive positions in their companies. While both take pride in their professional accomplishments, the achievement they each are most proud of is their family.

"I have a small but wonderful family," says Beverly Holmes. "I have a wise 83-year-old mother whom I adore, a daughter and son-in-law who are both successful in their respective fields, and my sister and family and all the new grandchildren; it is a great blessing to have family and good friends." On the personal side, she fulfilled her goal of retiring with her health and the financial security to do the things she enjoys.

"From a professional standpoint, I accomplished what I set out to do in reference to breaking the paradigm that a woman could not create, build, and grow a financially successful business—especially in a conservative financial services company," says Beverly. She received many accolades for her business accomplishment, including Mass-Mutual's President's Leadership Award.

Beverly says she is pleased with her ability to stay focused on her goals and her accomplishments and contributions to work, family, and friends. And last, but surely not least, she says she is "fulfilled through and in her faith in God knowing that she could not have accomplished all that she did on her own." Now, she says, she is looking forward to her next exciting adventure.

Monica Luechtefeld also starts with her family accomplishments when asked what she is most proud of having achieved. "I am extraordinarily proud of being a mom and having a wonderfully talented young man as my son, along with my gifted daughter-in-law, and two beautiful grandchildren. Family is very important to me, and I'm very proud to be Christopher's mom and Nana to Savanna and Trent."

From a professional perspective, Monica is proud of her role in creating Office Depot's Internet strategy and of the teams she has built. "It was incredibly exciting to take on a project where there was no road map, no book one could read or course one could take. The Internet was a totally new subject, so it was an opportunity to be both innovative and strategic. It was wonderful to build the Internet into a differentiator for the company and an important resource for our customers."

Monica also takes great pride in the accomplishments of the women and men she has had a chance to coach, mentor, and see advance into company leadership roles.

Plan for a Long Life
At different times in your life, success may look different. This is particularly true of your professional life.

You do not have to limit yourself to a traditional timeline that dictates that you need to start work right out of college and shoot up a trajectory to its pinnacle without a break. Today, with people living and working longer, women are recognizing that they have the flexibility to emphasize different aspects of their life at different times. There are more options than ever before. Plan for a long life. Everything does not have to happen simultaneously. In a profile on the Little PINK Book website, Anne Stevens, chairman, CEO, and principal at SA IT Services, says, "If you think of your life as 75-plus years and your career as 30-plus years, you can accomplish a lot. You just can't accomplish everything at one time."[4]

Sometimes you will place more emphasis on family life; sometimes you will place more emphasis on your professional life. You have to decide what you want to do and when. Some women have chosen to have a family early and a career later; others have focused on their career early and had a family later. Many have decided to do both simultaneously. You do not need to focus exclusively on one or the other.

While your family is young, you may prefer to work with a more flexible schedule and then focus in on your career as the children get older. Karen Wimbish, Director of Retail Retirement at Wells Fargo, says in a profile on the Glass Hammer website that she is a "second-half champion." Although she worked while her children were young, her career only took off after they were in high school. She says she never managed anyone until she was over 40; today she manages hundreds of people. "I don't believe in career paths—I believe in opportunities."[15]

Design Your Work around Your Life

This new approach women take to planning careers is supported and facilitated by changes in the way we work. For close to 100 years, people have been designing their lives around work. This mindset is what has contributed to the conflicts women have faced when building a professional career while also trying to have a fulfilling family life.

Today, both women and men are designing work around their lives. Many corporations are creating more flexible workplace policies as a result. This new mindset dramatically changes the potential and the possibilities for women. It offers a level of flexibility and choice that has never before been available and is opening up new opportunities for both women and men. For women in particular, flexibility allows them to manage the integration of professional and family goals. Having options allows women to remain active in the workforce while taking care of young children or other family responsibilities. It opens up new possibilities and potential to lead a fulfilling life. You will read more about the process of integrating your family and professional lives in Success Strategy Seven.

As women's definitions of professional success break free of the traditional definitions of moving up a defined career ladder as quickly as possible, they are viewing success through a different lens. They see success as what they will achieve over their career's lifetime. Their definition of professional success is much broader than what they can achieve within a single organization.

Kathe Albrecht says defining success in her own terms has been extremely important to her, in particular because she is in a position where advancement is not up the narrow ladder at the university where she works. Certainly leading the Visual Resources Center at American University is part of her professional definition of success. Early on she defined success as going beyond the successful Visual Resources Center at American University to include being a leader and influencing change in her profession. She went outside the university and became involved in national projects to develop standards for museum image use in universities and became president of her professional association. "That helped define my career," says Kathe. "I became known as someone who knew about the larger issues for the profession, but specifically as an expert in copyright and fair use of museum images."

Consider a Portfolio Career
Careers no longer have to be linear. An emerging concept is the portfolio career. Portfolio careers differ from a traditional career in that you are not working for one corporation, progressing up their predefined career ladder. Rather, it is a tapestry of positions and opportunities that you weave for yourself. The most successful portfolio careers are designed purposefully to expand your experiences, provide new opportunities, and build your reputation. You may choose to work for a series of organizations for relatively short periods of time or to offer your services as an independent consultant to multiple organizations simultaneously.

Today over a third of the workforce is composed of free agent contractors, providing services to companies from small to large. Carl T. Camden, president and CEO of Kelly Services, Inc., predicts this will grow to 50 percent over the next decade.[16] The importance of this trend for women is that these free agent positions are no longer limited to administrative positions; today they include lawyers, Ph.D. scientists and researchers, and even CEOs.

A portfolio career may be an option for a short period of time when you most require flexibility. It gives you the opportunity to maintain a high profile in your profession and keep your skills and expertise current while giving you maximum flexibility to manage your time and level of commitment. It also gives you an opportunity to gain diverse experiences that strengthen your credentials. After your circumstances change and your need for flexibility decreases, you have the option to move back into a traditional career, or a portfolio career may become your preferred career strategy.

For Kim Roberts, a portfolio career became her choice when she met and married an active duty Marine officer. She made the decision to move with him as his duty stations changed. With each move, she took advantage of opportunities in the area to add to her career and to her education. She says that despite the diversity in the jobs she has had, there has been a consistent theme. "My interests haven't changed; it's the venues in which I practice that have changed," says Kim. "I've been really lucky to see so much more than just the inside of one company. I think it is beneficial to the companies where I have worked too, because you come in with outside the box thinking."

However you use this option, these new ways of working give you ultimate control over your career, opening up choices and opportunities and avoiding gaps in your resume.

Take Advantage of the Benefits of Technology

Technology is one of the primary game changers in career flexibility. Technology facilitates communications anywhere anytime, making workplace flexibility a realistic option for women and men alike. The same technology that allows you to stay in touch with the office when you are traveling enables you to be productive while working at home or at different hours. Many companies are starting to offer flexible work arrangements and telecommuting.

Today the model where all employees and management are located in one central location has changed dramatically. At IBM, for example, Marilyn Johnson was based in Austin, Texas. Her boss was based in Armonk, New York. The people who reported to Marilyn were all around the country. They met by teleconference on a regular basis, communicated by e-mail, and kept in touch by cell phone when traveling.

Technology supports workplace flexibility, enabling both men and women to work from home, as well as in the office. At IBM, for example, many employees are home-based. They have access to a central work location where they can go for administrative support and meetings, or to work when they are traveling. However, their main office is based in their home.

Receiving job promotions and job changes no longer necessarily requires packing up and moving, thus avoiding all the family disloca-tion that often accompanies a move. With increasing globalization, senior managers are leading functions with locations around the world—and they can do that from anywhere.

Make Flexible Work Arrangements a Career Plus
The interpretation of flexible working arrangements is all in the posi-tioning. Some people may view those who using flextime as lacking career ambition and interest in progressing in the company. Reposition your desire for flexible work arrangements as a sign of your commit-ment to the company, your job, and your career. Make the case that rather than choosing to leave the company, you are seeking ways to con-tribute to your fullest capacity while also fulfilling your personal goals.

Develop a plan for flexible arrangements that takes into account the demands of your job and shows how you will be able to meet the position requirements, regardless of where you work. Look at your job creatively to identify ways you can take advantage of technology. Figure out what you can do just as effectively from home and what requires your presence in the office. A day devoted to answering e-mails, preparing a long report, and doing international phone calls may be done even more effectively from home than in the office. Make certain your boss and your employees know how to contact you when you are working remotely. Take the initiative to check in by phone or e-mail so they realize you are in touch and available to them. Take care that your use of flexibility does not result in addi-tional workload for your manager or your employees.

Make sure you still have the face time with your manager and other decision makers so they will think of you for special assignments and opportunities. Identify the times when it truly is important to be in the office. Be flexible if a situation requiring your presence comes up on a day you are not scheduled to be in the office. Make the case that working from home actually increases productivity because you are not spending two to three hours commuting.

Establish the Goals to Achieve Success

Your definition of success drives the goals you establish in each area of your life. Set high goals, goals that will challenge you and bring out your best. Make certain your goals are goals you want to achieve, goals that reflect your visions, values, and self-confidence. Be sure your goals are focused on your aspirations for the future and are not the reflection of past experiences. This is a time to open yourself up to all possibilities.

Establish goals in every sector of your life, goals that contribute to achieving your vision for your future and that complement and strengthen each other. Include all the important aspects of your life, and ensure that you will be able to enjoy both your job and your personal life. "You are not supposed to make your life a slave to your job or your work a slave to your life. Nor are you supposed to hate your job or your home life," says Kate Nealon. Look for ways to integrate the two. We will return to integrating the various aspects of your life in "Success Strategy Seven: Nurture Your Greatest Asset—You" with tools for making your goals a reality in Success Strategy Seven.

Get Ahead of the Trends

The way we work has changed dramatically over the past 20 years, and what we see today is only the tip of the iceberg. With increasing globalization and expanding technological solutions to dispersed styles of working together, the world of work will continue to change at an unprecedented rate. This is a tremendous advantage for you. Since you are not entrenched in the traditional paths to success, it is easier for you to anticipate the trends, identify new paths that may fit your overall goals better than the traditional ones, and pursue success in multiple ways.

Give Your Plan a Periodic Review

Just as you give your employees a regular review of their successes and areas for improvement, you need to do a regular review of your life strategy. Go back to your strategy on a regular schedule. Some women tell us they do this every year; others do it at longer intervals—every five or ten years.

Your life strategy is not carved in marble. It is an organic plan that will change as you change and grow. As life "happens," you may find your strategy maturing and evolving, your priorities shifting, and your goals becoming clearer. Review your achievements, assess your personal development, and analyze how your experiences have affected your strategy. Achieving your life's dreams requires constant refinement and improvement. Some find that when they have had major "aha" moments or important experiences, they automatically reflect on their strategy and begin the process of making changes. Remember, it's YOUR future—so revise it, update it, and, most of all, make it the driving force of your life.

Success is not a destination; it is a continuous journey with peaks of joyous achievement and valleys of sloughing along just trying to keep going. There always will be choices to be made. Sometimes there will be success in one facet of your life and not in others. True success comes from believing in yourself and your ability to achieve all that you aspire to be.

Define Success in Your Own Terms: In Summary

- Know yourself.
  - Define your values and live by them.
  - Find your passion.
  - Inventory your strengths and weaknesses.
- Define success
  - Develop your guiding vision.
  - Think holistically.
  - Plan for a long life.

- Design your work around your life.
  - Consider a portfolio career.
  - Take advantage of the benefits of technology
  - Make flexible work arrangements a career plus.
- Establish the goals to achieve success.
- Get ahead of the trends.
- Give your plan a periodic review.

Be the Architect of Your Career

Building a career takes a little serendipity; a bit of being in the right place at the right time; a considerable amount of flexibility, courage, and belief in yourself; and a lot of risk taking and hard work. Most important of all, it involves taking responsibility for propelling yourself to achieve your goals. No matter how prominent your sponsors or how wide-ranging your networks, at the core of professional success is having the skills and the experience to apply those skills, to expand your portfolio, and to demonstrate your capabilities.

A prevailing myth believed by many people is that you can plan your career from day one and then pursue it. In reality, careers are flexible and often unpredictable. It is critical to think through and develop your professional goals. Take into account your goals in the other aspects of your life—especially family and personal goals—and consider how they integrate with, and influence, each other. Realize that the influence of family and personal goals on your professional goals will vary depending on the stage of your life.

Professional experiences, both at work and in industry organizations, are likely to have a profound impact on your professional goals. As you have new experiences and are exposed to different aspects of business, you will learn what intrigues you; as a result, your professional goals and interests will become more targeted. You may aim to move into different aspects of the business or of your industry. You may decide to specialize further in your original area. Like many women, as you move into middle management, you may become more attracted to being in senior management. Women in middle management are 20 percent more likely to say they aspire to a role in their organization's leadership than those in entry-level positions. Twenty-two percent of women in middle management say senior management roles are worth the cost compared to only 14 percent of those in entry-level positions.[1] Once being in a senior-level position becomes your goal, it will drive your career plan.

Marilyn Johnson says it was when she learned that the executive ranks shape business strategy that she decided she wanted to be an executive. "Strategy informs the direction of the corporation, and that affects profit and return on investment and stockholder protection. I wanted to be integral to that process," says Marilyn. "So from the day I knew about the executive ranks, I aspired to get there. Once you know your goal, the next step is to think about how to get there."

Career Progression Is Not a Straight Track

Career progression is almost never a straight track. Often what seems like a detour ends up becoming your passion. Most of the women interviewed for this book started out expecting their career would take them in one direction, but ended up doing something totally different and loving it. Their early experiences were often driven by necessity, contacts, or chance. They learned what they enjoyed doing and where they could excel. This led to new opportunities, which in turn resulted in their finding their passion and a career that was professionally and personally energizing and meaningful. They achieved their success because they were open to the possibilities, willing to try something unexpected and different, and able to turn every situation into an opportunity for learning and professional growth.

Monica Luechtefeld's journey to becoming a senior executive at Office Depot is an excellent example. Monica earned her degree in biology and expected that would be her career direction. She finished her degree requirements a semester early and, while waiting to graduate, took a job in the college admissions office doing college relations and student recruiting. She enjoyed it so much that she decided to stay on after graduation, ultimately becoming director of admissions for the college. Although she loved the position, it required weekend and evening hours plus on-call availability to parents and students. When she decided to start a family, Monica reluctantly decided to seek a position with less impact on her personal time. When a close family friend who had an office products and supply company offered her a job, she accepted, redirecting her career. This move ultimately resulted in her becoming one of the leaders in transforming the office supplies industry and to her current position as executive vice president at Office Depot.

Susan Helstab, like Monica Luechtefeld, was a biology major. Susan expected to teach after graduation, but teaching jobs were scarce. She quickly realized she was not enjoying the jobs she could find and decided to go back to school to get an advanced degree. It was late in the year, and the only program she could enter in January was business school. "I went to business school simply because that was where I could be back at school," says Susan with a smile in her voice. She fell in love with business, and since she had a quantitative background from her biology studies, she decided to major in finance. With her first marketing class, she discovered a new passion, and graduated with a joint specialization in finance and marketing. Having both specializations opened up a wide range of opportunities from banking to advertising. She chose to join an advertising firm. When Four Seasons Hotels and Resorts approached her about a position in marketing, she made the decision to move and began a 25-year career that has taken her to the top levels of company leadership.

Marilyn Johnson was a broadcaster and a schoolteacher before she accepted a position at IBM and found a direction that led to her becoming a global executive for IBM. Judy Robinson originally worked in an international marketing company. But it was not until she joined the U.S. Army that she found her passion.

Sometimes the right position does not come along immediately.

Build relationships with recruiters, managers at companies you are interested in joining, and people in your network who can provide referrals. Keep in touch by checking in, seeing how they are doing, and reiterating your interests. In the meantime, gain experience and build your reputation for achieving results in other jobs. People—whether recruiters or mentors—like to refer and hire winners.

Persistence pays off. Camye Mackey knew she wanted a career in human resources, but when she graduated, there weren't many HR openings available. "I knew the importance of networking, so I kept the recruiter's business cards from the major organizations that I interviewed with on my college campus," says Camye. "I would call the recruiter from the company I was most interested in every six months to ensure that he knew of my continued interest and to ask if there were any opportunities in human resources." The relationship paid off two years later when the recruiter called to ask if she was still interested in a position at Walt Disney World.

Ignore the Rules

In business following the rules can slow your progress. Women often believe that you succeed by following the rules and doing what you are told. Karen Wimbish, Director of Retail Retirement at Wells Fargo, says she wishes she had been less intent on following the rules. Leaders take risks, seek out challenging assignments, are flexible, and consistently innovate. They move horizontally as well as up the hierarchy. They create their own path. "I was very much a follower," says Karen Wimbish. "But progressing in your career is not about following the rules. There's no syllabus to getting ahead, and I had to stretch in ways that were uncomfortable to me."[2]

Go beyond accepted wisdom about the correct way to do things. Where others see barriers, the most successful women see opportunities. Where others believe the best way to accomplish a goal is the proven way, successful women leaders believe there may be a different, better process, and they set out to find and implement it.

We asked successful women business leaders what they did to

gain the experience and credentials they needed to achieve their goals. Rather than following a route prescribed by tradition, they sought out ways to gain experience, expand their horizons, and stand out as innovators and leaders who make things happen. They made certain that they learned about the company's operations, finances, and strategic directions as well as getting to know the right people. While they followed paths of their own creation, they also pointed out that there are some credentials that are foundational, that you cannot ignore. In this chapter, we share with you both—the basics and the options. Not every action works for every career; use these recommendations as a foundation for designing your personalized career path and achieving your aspirations.

Choose the Right Place to Work

Whether you are transitioning between companies or just starting out, go beyond the position being offered and take time to analyze the company's values, culture, and management styles. If these factors align with your personal values, you are more likely to be in a position to grow and advance.

Recognize That the Company Culture Is More Important Than the Position

Investigate the culture of the company you are considering joining. Don't allow the attraction of a specific opportunity blind you to the importance of the culture. Jobs can change, but cultures remain constant. Monica Luechtefeld says, "Choose a company to work for based on how well its values match your values. The values of the company are more important than the specific job you are being offered."

Make certain the company is one where you will be proud to say you work there, where you will enjoy going to work every day, and where there is potential for you to grow, learn, advance, and flourish. Maria Coyne says, "It was important to me to join a company whose values reflected my personal values. To this day, that is the reason I stay at the bank."

Too many women do not appreciate the importance of the fit between their values and the organization. Susan Helstab says that at the start of her career, "I didn't appreciate how important the values of an organization were going to be to me. Now, when I give career advice, it is to identify the goodness of fit between your personal values and the values of the organization."

For some people, the culture and opportunities at a smaller company or an entrepreneurial start-up may provide the career development and personal development they are seeking. You could do this to launch your career or later in your career as a growth opportunity. Smaller companies can provide a great training ground at any point in your career. You are likely to be given more responsibility earlier, work more closely with the top management from the beginning, and have a greater opportunity to make an impact on the strategic direction of the business than you would have in a large corporation. As your career progresses, joining a smaller company can offer challenges and opportunities for personal growth not as readily available in a large organization. Joining a small company also can carry a higher level of risk. Pay and benefits may not be as generous, and there is a greater potential that the company could go out of business. You have to be ready to accept the potential risks as well as the rewards.

However, the career advancement you achieve can position you for more senior positions, if you move to a larger organization. It can also bring substantial personal wealth if you have received stock in lieu of higher salary and the company goes public.

Sheryl Sandberg, Chief Operating Officer of Facebook and number 12 on *Fortune* magazine's list of the "100 Most Powerful Women," says her priority in pursuing a job is the opportunity it affords her for personal growth. She found the best opportunities for growth were in smaller companies where she could influence the company's growth strategies and, not inconsequentially, build personal wealth.

Sheryl is a graduate of the Harvard Business School, where she got to know Larry Summers, who was on the faculty. After college, she worked for McKinsey & Company. When Larry Summers became U.S. Secretary of the Treasury, she was his Chief of Staff. When she left government, she moved to Silicon Valley, where she was attracted to the opportunities offered by a small, three-year-old company called Google. She was willing to accept the risk that came with this opportunity. At Google, she identified new market opportunities for the company and created, from scratch, its game-changing global online sales operation. Ready for a new challenge after six years at Google, she started exploring options both inside the company and with other organizations.

Although Sheryl was in discussions with several large corporations, she was intrigued when Mark Zuckerberg, the founder of Facebook, called. What was important to her was to work with someone whose values she shared and to have an opportunity to create something that did not exist. She saw in the growth potential of the social media company a new career challenge and a personal growth opportunity. Once again, she was willing to take the risks that come with joining a young start-up. So despite offers to join established enterprises, she moved to Facebook, where she reported to the 26-year-old founder of a company that was bleeding cash. Today, having created the strategy for making the company highly profitable, she is a key player in taking Facebook public. What attracted her first to Google and then to Facebook was the opportunity to be instrumental in transforming the companies into profitable, international, high-growth enterprises.[3]

In the final analysis, the most important consideration is not the size of the company but whether the company's culture is one that will allow you to contribute to at your highest level, encourage you to grow, and help you to develop. One of the reasons Sheryl Sandberg gave for joining Facebook was that it was a company driven by instinct and human relations. Use your values as the filter to make your decision. If you have any doubts about the organization, do not get carried away by the opportunity of a single job.

Learn If the Company Values Women

The role of women in the company is an important signal about the culture and what opportunities you may be given. In evaluating a company, take into account whether it is a company that provides opportunity and support for women and values their contribution at the leadership level across the business. Look at how many women there are in senior positions. What functions do women head? Are women leading primarily in staff functions, such as human resources and administrative support, or are there women executives in sales, technology, legal, and finance? Are women in positions where they are responsible for strategic profit and loss centers? Are they in executive positions that influence the company's future direction?

If there already are women in senior leadership positions, it is more likely that you will have the opportunity for growth and advancement. You are less likely to have to break down barriers to advance. The presence of women leaders in key business areas tells you the company takes seriously the value of women as business leaders. This opens up more opportunities for you.

Having women in place at all levels in the organization, especially in managerial leadership roles, provides female role models so you do not have to figure out from scratch how to lead like a woman and how to navigate the power structure. It means you have access to a pool of highly successful women who can become mentors or sponsors.

Check out the number of women on the board of directors as well as in internal leadership positions. Women on boards often are the ones who focus on the advancement of women in the company and on flexible work arrangements. They often take the time to meet with internal women's groups to learn about the culture and the climate for women in the company.

Review the company's record on recruiting and retaining women. Is there a company women's network, and is it taken seriously? Women's networks are one of the signals that a company takes women seriously and promotes their career growth. It is a plus for you because a strong women's network provides opportunities to meet and learn from women leaders across the company, as well as to meet and network with senior leaders, opportunities often not available within the day-to-day work context.

Investigate the Company's Commitment to Employees

Look at the total compensation package, including salary, bonuses, health insurance, education, vacation, sick leave, stock purchase opportunities, and retirement plan. Obtain as much information as you can about salaries, how they are set, and how the salary review process works. Ask about the performance evaluation process and how it relates to compensation. Understand your options for contributing to the retirement plan. The more senior you are, the more complex the total compensation package becomes—including stock options, bonuses, and other forms of performance-based compensation. Don't be reluctant to seek out professional advice on the best package for you.

Compare the total compensation package with industry averages and with comparable companies. If the package is not commensurate with the plans in similar companies, find out why.

Find out if the company offers internal education programs, from skills training to keep you abreast of the latest trends to ongoing management development. For example, when Sharon was at IBM, managers were required to attend 40 hours of management training every year. As a result, she received a world-class education in management and leadership, and became more adept at leading people. A strong commitment to employee development provides insights into company values about its people.

Also check out the company's educational benefits, such as tuition refund for pursuing an advanced degree or specialized technical or professional training. This can be valuable to you if you find you want to strengthen your credentials. For executives, take a look at the executive education options the company offers and what is required to qualify for these opportunities.

Find out about workplace flexibility policies and practices and see if employees are comfortable taking advantage of these policies. If the position you are considering requires regular travel, check out the company's travel policies.

Understand the Company's Reputation in Its Industry

Find out about the company's reputation in its markets and its record for innovation. A company that has good customer relations probably has strong values of customer service, product quality, and leadership in its industry. A company's commitment to innovation provides the basis for continued operational success and for increased opportunities for employees.

Review the company's financial performance. Is it consistently profitable? What are its prospects for growth? Growth creates new opportunities for employees. These are all indicators of the company's health and the likelihood it will be there for the long run.

Research local, national, and industry news reports about the company and its business. Go beyond the formal interview process and look for informal opportunities, such as conferences or professional association events, to meet company employees from the administrative to the executive levels, as well as customers and community leaders who work with the company. Talk to people who work at the company or who have worked there to learn about the company culture, their opinions about the company, and the opportunities the company affords its employees for professional growth.

Realize the Manager Is the Key to Your Success

Whether you are transitioning to a new company or just starting out, your manager is the key to your success. As you investigate the company, see what you can learn about the company's management style and the experience of the person to whom you will report. Learn as much as you can about the manager's track record with hiring, developing, and promoting women. Will you be the only woman reporting to this person? Especially if you are coming in at a senior level, what are the manager's prospects for advancement? How influential is she or he in the leadership of the company?

Share your aspirations with the manager and see how she or he responds. Ask about development opportunities, both within the department and in the company in general. Bring up questions that will provide insight into the manager's values, goals for the organization, and management style. Ask how the manager expects you to contribute to the success of the business unit. If possible, meet with other employees in the group. If you are replacing another employee, see if you can talk to the incumbent. Trust your instincts to tell you if this will be a good fit for you and if you and the manager will make a team that will be successful for both of you and for the company.

Choose the Right Place: In Summary

- Recognize that the company culture is more important than the position.
- Learn if the company values women.
- Investigate the company's commitment to employees.
- Understand the company's reputation in its industry.
- Realize that the manager is the key to your success.

The Basics of Building a Strong Foundation

The advice in this section is focused on building a strong foundation, no matter what direction your career takes. The recommendations in this section are nonnegotiable; they are fundamental to business success of every kind. If you do nothing else suggested in this chapter, the recommendations in this section are the ones you must embrace and act upon.

Focus on Results and Outcomes

Successful women do not just complete assignments; they create results that are sustainable, are measurable, and contribute to the strategic goals of the organization. Focus on delivering measurable outcomes. Senior management is looking for results.

Become known as a person who overcomes barriers and makes things happen. Develop a reputation for being the go-to person for the tough assignments that others are unwilling, or afraid, to undertake.

When these assignments come along, your first reaction should be, "I'll figure it out." Organizations value people whose analyses, planning, and execution result in attaining goals, not in providing reasons something cannot be done. If something truly is not possible, successful women identify alternative strategies that achieve the results your executives are seeking. Present your proposed alternatives with the supporting business case and then deliver on your commitment.

Learn the business of your organization, how your company makes money, and how your area of the business contributes to what the whole business has to deliver to its customers and shareholders. Measure, measure, measure. In business, if you cannot measure it, it does not happen, or if it does happen, there is no basis for evaluating it. Understand what results management expects from your function and establish metrics to track and report progress against these results. In addition to financial measurements, develop measurements of key activities and processes. Metrics help both you and your employees track progress, evaluate business performance, and be forewarned when something is not working. When you are presenting your group's results to management, use these metrics and connect them to the company's overall business goals. Success Strategy Five, "Translate the Stories Numbers Tell to Drive Strategic Results," provides more in-depth knowledge and tools to ensure you can excel in this area.

Debra Hanna is the associate director of the Critical Path to TB Drug Consortium at the Critical Path Institute and the former senior principal scientist, laboratory head, and project team leader for antibacterial research at Pfizer Worldwide Research. She says that her focus on outcomes was critical to her advancement. "Understanding how our science was connected to the highest-level corporate outcomes, and then becoming outcomes-focused in all that I did, was incredibly important to my advancement at Pfizer. Being outcomes-focused was also a key factor in securing my new position at the Critical Path Institute."

Know what outcomes are required for your department to contribute to the health of your function, your division, and the company overall and deliver on them consistently. Virginia Rometty, the first woman to be named CEO of IBM, is known for always delivering on the results. "You can't argue with that," says Patti Ross, President, Patricia Ross & Associates, and former Marketing Executive, Women's Global Market at IBM.

It Is about Face Time

No matter how good your outcomes are, being visible to the decision makers is critical. When your results are being presented to senior management, ask to be the one who presents them. Make certain you are recognized as the one who was responsible for delivering the results. When your manager is presenting the division's annual plan to senior management, ask to be part of the presentation.

Make certain you are in the meetings where issues and decisions concerning your function are discussed or where your expertise and experience can contribute to the overall organizational decision. Even today, women may still be left out. While this is usually not intentional, meetings may be scheduled very early in the morning, making it difficult for you to get there if you have school-age children, or on a day when you normally work from home.

Take advantage of informal conversations with senior management to demonstrate your understanding of current issues the company is facing or provide an update on your function's contributions to business success. Perhaps you have feedback from a customer who is pleased that a new process you introduced has reduced turnaround time by 20 percent; use the few moments you have to update the executive.

If you are left out of critical meetings, address the issue in a calm, professional manner. "You made a decision that impacts my business and my people, and I was not there to provide my input on the implications of these decisions." Addressing the issue often is sufficient to prevent it from happening again.

Seek out opportunities to demonstrate your capabilities, to learn about your business, and to work with senior management. Volunteer for task forces or special assignments that will expand your experience while providing visibility with leaders in different parts of your company, as well as in your industry. Be the one who presents the findings or leads the discussions so you become recognized as a leader who is making things happen and delivering results.

Position Yourself for the Future

Deep in their hearts, many women still want to believe the business world is a meritocracy, and if they do a good job, they will be recognized, rewarded, and promoted. They focus on doing their current job as well as possible in anticipation of recognition and promotion. Build on your performance as demonstrated by your business outcomes to make yourself known as a high-potential candidate for other opportunities.

View your current position as the launching pad for the future. Men are very good at using their present job to carefully position themselves for the next job or for future promotion. Performing in your current position is indeed important, *but* you also need to focus on positioning yourself for the future, whether pursuing a specific job you have identified or simply being ready when an unexpected opportunity comes along.

Determine what experience, skills, and education are necessary for key opportunities. Identify actions you can take to demonstrate you have the qualifications and experience to be a viable candidate for higher-level positions and to attract high-level sponsors. Analyze what you can do in your current job that demonstrates your potential for the next level of responsibility.

Make certain your manager and other leaders know of your interests and aspirations. When a position becomes available, ask the hiring manager for an informational interview to learn about the position and make the manager aware of your interest and credentials. If there is a position you would like, toss your hat in the ring. Build the business case and ask for the promotion. If it is not a job you would like, at least you have learned more about the business, refined your aspirations, and gained visibility with a senior manager who may later have an opening for which you would be perfect.

Learn and Let Go

At each stage of your career, you draw on the full range of your expertise and capabilities and expand your knowledge and skills. At the same time, one of the most important things you learn to do is to figure out how to let go of those activities that no longer are appropriate for your role.

Early in your career, your focus will be mainly on individual efforts and participation as part of a team. As you progress, you may assume the role of team leader, overseeing and integrating the work of other team members. Your job increasingly becomes one of achieving goals through the efforts of others. This will require you to let go of the mindset that you have to do everything yourself for it to be successful. You will need to develop an entirely new set of skills— learning to break projects down into assignments, delegating to the appropriate staff members, and overseeing the quality and integration of all the assignments.

You will repeat this process at each level as you progress. Learning to let go of the work that made you successful in your previous position can be challenging—especially those parts where you really excel and that you most enjoy doing. When you move into a new position, especially at more senior levels, compare the responsibilities of your new position with those of your previous position. Analyze what you did in the previous position, how you spent your time, and what skills were required. Contrast that with the new position. Identify the new skills you need, figure out what is critical to achieving success in the new position, and determine how you need to apportion your time. Identify how your performance will be evaluated and what top management expects from this position. Understand what activities now are inappropriate for you to continue, regardless of your proficiency at them. Consciously decide that these activities need to go.

You will repeat this process over and over again, whether you are making a lateral move or progressing up the hierarchy. Learn all you can from each position, add to your knowledge base, and move on!

Be Comfortable Being Uncomfortable

Remember this advice from Success Strategy Two, "Own Your Destiny." It is such a vital and recurring theme that we have repeated it here. Learning new skills and dealing with change is usually uncomfortable and often frustrating. It is hard to transition from a position where you understand the issues, can readily make the best decisions, and know all the stakeholders who are affected by your actions. It is very similar to the transition from high school to college. Suddenly you are in a new environment and have to learn how to be successful all over again. Yet it is a critical part of learning and growing. In fact, the opportunity to learn is a compelling reason for seeking out and taking on new positions. Embrace that feeling of uncertainty, use your "figure it out smarts," and seek advice from your mentors. "Never turn down an opportunity because you think you are not ready for it," say the most successful businesswomen. Trust yourself and go for it.

The Basics of Building a Strong Foundation: In Summary

- Focus on results and outcomes.
- It is about face time.
- Position yourself for the future.
- Learn and let go.
- Be comfortable being uncomfortable.

The Building Blocks

Move into People Management ASAP

While it is important to earn your spurs by doing a terrific technical job, move as quickly as possible from being a top technician to being a manager. Take advantage of opportunities where you can lead teams. "Never turn down an opportunity to lead people because the people perspective is really the bang for the buck," says Judy Robinson.

As you advance in your career, leadership skills and experience become much more important than technical skills. Senior management is looking for the leaders who can rally a lot of people from diverse areas of the business to achieve a big goal. Gain a reputation for building and leading high-performing teams that achieve top results for the business. Become known as someone who can coalesce functions from across the business into joining you in solving an organizational challenge or creating a new market. These are the skills that management values; these are the skills that distinguish you and make you a candidate for promotions and high-visibility positions.

Get Profit-and-Loss Responsibility Early

It is imperative to get profit-and-loss (P&L) responsibility as early as possible in your career. A common explanation for why women do not get the top leadership positions is that they have not held jobs with P&L responsibility. The critical importance of P&L experience was highlighted in a recent *Wall Street Journal* article, "More Women Are Primed to Land CEO Roles." The article cites the lack of profit-and-loss experience as a key barrier to women's progress to the top leadership jobs. At Campbell Soup Co. there were four women among CEO Douglas Conant's direct reports when he was selecting his successor. But only one of them, Denise Morrison, had P&L experience. She got the job.[4] No one can deny your results when you can show them a P&L statement that proves you are leading a profitable, growing operation.

Profit-and-loss experience gives you the opportunity to understand the financial structure of your company, what drives profitability, and how to successfully deploy resources. It teaches you how your decisions, no matter how small, can impact the bottom-line results of your business unit and, ultimately, the company's bottom line. Successfully leading an organization with P&L responsibility is the best way to demonstrate you have the judgment and business skills to lead a profitable business that contributes to the organization's bottom-line results. This is a vital credential; just get it.

"You need to have P&L experience as soon as possible in your career, even if it's a small job, in order to be prepared for promotions and larger opportunities that come along later in your career," says Monica Luechtefeld. "P&L responsibility is crucial to advance to senior positions in an organization."

Even if you see your career in staff areas such as human resources or communications, seek out assignments in areas that will give you P&L experience and credentials. You will be more effective in a senior staff position if you have the credibility that comes from successfully managing P&L areas, and you will have a better understanding of the impact of your decisions and actions on the business.

Go International

International experience increasingly is required to qualify for many senior positions today. The world is transitioning from an American century in business to a global century in business, reports the dean of the Harvard Business School.[5] Most businesses today, regardless of size or industry, operate internationally. As a result, they are managing diverse, cross-national employees, customers, suppliers, competitors, and creditors. As companies are seeking expansion opportunities, they are moving beyond national boundaries to benefit from growing economies. For example, the fastest-growing markets in the world as of this writing are the BRIC countries—Brazil, Russia, India, and China.[6]

Corporations need executives with global mindsets and cross-cultural sensitivity. Yet, the pool of executives with global leadership experience is not keeping up with the demand. Eighty-five percent of Fortune 500 companies have reported a shortage of global leaders with the necessary International skills.[7]

This is a tremendous opportunity for women. Because they are sensitive to individual differences and diverse customers, their skills at creating inclusive environments position them to be effective working in cultures outside their own.

As a project leader or manager, increasingly women are likely to be working with or managing internal departments located in multiple countries, creating alliances with suppliers outside their country, developing international markets, or establishing operations outside the United States. Opportunities for advancement are wide open for those who have the experience and the track record in working globally.

Seek out special projects that include an international component and give you experience with the business cultures, customs, and values outside your home country. If possible, take an overseas assignment. Having direct experience in the dynamics of global relationships and operations is becoming the tipping point between you and other candidates for senior leadership positions.

Recognize That Education Pays

Over three-quarters of the women we interviewed have advanced degrees, and quite a few have multiple graduate degrees. In addition to MBAs, they also have professional degrees or certifications in their fields. While a graduate degree is usually not a required qualification for a CEO, 42 percent of the Fortune 100 chief executives have an MBA or a master's degree in finance or economics.

Women benefit from having a master's degree in business administration or an advanced professional degree, according to Elissa Sangster, Executive Director of the Forté Foundation, which focuses on educating and preparing women for business leadership.[8] Advanced degrees provide skills and knowledge that you need to be successful in the business world. Plus they translate into dollars. In the United States, a master's degree results in a 23 percent higher salary than a bachelor's degree; a professional degree results in a 55 percent higher salary than a bachelor's degree.[9]

In addition to gaining knowledge and skills, pursuing an advanced degree gives you a very strong network of influential business and community leaders. Most advanced degree programs move students through in a cohort, which fosters close ties. You will find your fellow students become colleagues over the years and provide an ongoing support network. They are very likely to be the leaders of the future and can be a source of connections, mentors, and sponsors.

The Building Blocks: In Summary

- Move into people management ASAP.
- Get profit-and-loss responsibility early.
- Go international.
- Recognize that education pays.

Options and Opportunities

The business world offers a variety of opportunities to make a difference and position yourself for success, all the while having fun. This section presents proven options for earning the credentials to be considered for executive leadership. Most have the benefit of high visibility. None are without risks. However, even taking risk can create credibility for you as an innovative leader who has the capacity to influence the direction and health of the company.

Seek Out Lattice Assignments

Today, corporations recognize that leaders need to have diverse experiences that span all parts of the corporation. In addition, organizations are becoming flatter. Over the past 20 years, organizations have become 25 percent flatter, which means there are fewer levels of hierarchy and, therefore, fewer options for moving straight up.[10]

Historically, high-potential women and men have focused on career progression as moving up a vertical ladder with clearly defined criteria for achieving each level. Today, often, the best way to the top is to move horizontally or diagonally

This strategy has been termed a "lattice career." For a visual image of what a lattice career is, envision the trellis that a gardener uses to support flowering vines. The beauty of the career lattice is it can extend infinitely in any direction. You can move horizontally, diagonally, or straight up.

A lattice career strategy offers a path to broaden your experience, learn about new areas, gain exposure to leaders from different parts of the company, and explore new career paths. Seek out lateral moves within your own company or when moving to another company. Leadership skills are transferable. Identify diagonal moves that will allow you to learn a new area of the business or gain experience in other parts of your industry while applying the leadership skills you already have developed.

Similar to any other move to a new area, you are taking a risk and you have to deliver, but the experience and the credentials you will gain make it worthwhile. Senior executives value people who are able to move nimbly across the business functions, deliver results in diverse parts of the company, and therefore have a broad understanding of the entire company and its businesses.

Transform Your Organization

Be an initiator of change, not a follower. Use your time as a department manager to develop and demonstrate your skills at creating a world-class organization that contributes to the success of the business.

It is easy when you take over a successful department to just ratchet up performance and continue to operate it as in the past. However, with the rate of change in today's businesses, a complacent department soon becomes an out-of-date department. The most successful women have not been satisfied with maintaining the status quo. They envision the department of the future. They constantly seek to improve on an already high standard of products and services. They create a culture of innovation to retain and delight clients and attract new clients. They look at their internal relationships and seek to improve the interface with other departments. They ask if the department is making the greatest contribution it can to the success of the business. They ask questions about the possibilities:

- Why do we do it this way?
- Is there a better way?
- In the best of all worlds, what would we be doing and how would we do it?

They make changes to leapfrog ahead of the curve and be ready for emerging challenges.

Take, for example, Kathe Albrecht. When she took over as Curator of the Visual Resources Center at American University, the center was a slide library. She recognized that technology was transforming the use of visual images and that her department had the potential to become a leading pioneer in the field, contributing to both its value to the university and its reputation in the industry. As a result of her leadership, the Visual Resources Center was transformed. She guided the transition from analog to digital visual information. She expanded its relationships with internal departments so it is now sought after to participate in university-wide projects and is viewed as a prestigious resource to be included in grants. With Kathe's leadership, the Visual Resources Center has become an industry model and has enhanced American University's reputation.

Take the initiative to put your department at the leading edge of using technology to transform operations. Evaluate new technologies and develop new competencies to improve your department's performance and contribute to the company's profitability.

Become a resource for other parts of the business. Be market driven and constantly evaluate the status of your market and customers. Enhance existing markets and create new markets. "Be first and be lonely in the market," advises Virginia Rometty.[11]

Examine how your department works internally with other departments. Identify ways to improve collaboration, increase efficiency, and be more responsive to each other internally. Develop collaborative relationships with other departments to increase efficiency and effectiveness by adopting new ways of working together or implementing new technologies.

Take on Turnaround Projects

Many women advise volunteering for the jobs that no one else wants, especially turnarounds. Executives value leaders who know how to deal with adversity. Leading a successful organization only shows that you can maintain an already well-run operation. Taking on an existing operation that is faltering and turning it into a successful one provides more interesting challenges and provides you with a greater learning opportunity.

One of the best ways to learn how to build a successful business is to study businesses that fail. Use the opportunity to learn from what went wrong, both to figure out what needs to be changed in this particular situation and to learn what goes into building a successful business. Analyze the problems and determine what must be changed to turn the operation around. Build on all the resources available to you, including employees in the function who may understand the problem better than anyone else, as well as mentors and sponsors. While the risks are high, the results are worth it. Leading a turnaround operation is usually a high-visibility opportunity, which provides you with the opportunity to showcase your strengths, gain credibility as a business leader, and earn a reputation for making a difference.

Become an "Intrapreneur"

An "intrapreneur" is an entrepreneur within a large organization. Similar to entrepreneurs, intrapreneurs envision new opportunities for the company. Intrapreneurship can take the shape of building a new business within your business or reinventing an existing business function.

Identify new opportunities for your company, such as being the first mover in an emerging industry trend. Look for ways to apply new technologies, create new markets, meet competition, or develop new solutions in response to emerging external or internal challenges. These cannot be "would-be-good-to-do" ideas; they must be substantial business opportunities with bottom-line advantage to the company's profitability. You must prepare yourself to present a persuasive business case and advocate for the concept.

Think big when you do this. Small changes may enhance your performance; big changes will transform your future. Building a new business takes vision, persistence, and courage. This does not happen overnight, and you have to continue to be an advocate for your idea, selling and reselling it.

Look for those "once in a lifetime opportunities to create a career where none existed before and grow it to become a significant part of the business," says Monica Luechtefeld. For Monica, this kind of opportunity came in 1993, when she was invited to MIT for a presentation about the Internet as a new business tool. Convinced that the Internet would transform the way business was done and that Office Depot should be a first mover into the space, she built the business case, gained the support of the CEO, and led the development of the business application for Internet sales. Similar to an entrepreneur, she had to create the market for the new product. So she spent two years crisscrossing the country, meeting with customers to educate them on the Internet and the benefits of this new technology. "It took two long years to acquire the first 500 online customers," says Monica. "The next year we had about 11,000 connected and then 40,000 and today the Office Depot's Internet platform is international, with 50 websites, in 20 languages, and connecting millions of customers all over the world."

An intrapreneur's visions often are transformational. She or he sees opportunities where others do not. She or he engages existing company resources as well as brings in resources with skills and expertise that do not exist in the company. Similar to an entrepreneur, an intrapreneur figures out how to turn opportunities into thriving businesses, develop business plans, gain the support of management, and lead development.

Because you are competing for corporate resources, you must build a compelling business case for your idea, showing the projected value of the project to the company as well as the investment required to launch it.

The internal challenges are not over even when you have senior management's approval. You have to continue to be an advocate for your vision and engage others in supporting it. Do not expect everyone to cheer you on when you are trying to introduce a new way of doing business. There will be skeptics who won't believe in your new business model, no matter how strong a business case you have made. One woman who had been given the go-ahead to develop a new market for her company found that there still were internal barriers to moving ahead. Managers of other functions often were slow to respond to requests for support or questioned the need for what she had requested. Be prepared for this. Women who have been intrapreneurs say part of being an intrapreneur is developing your strategies for dealing with these barriers to success. Often being creative in finding ways to work around them is a better solution than escalating the issue. But recognize when the only option is to be forceful in overcoming obstacles and address them with management.

Even your friends may say you are wasting your time and talents on a wild goose chase. Monica Luechtefeld says with a smile, "Today, those same people come up to me and say, 'Thank God you didn't listen to us and kept going.'"

Become an Entrepreneur

Women have been starting businesses at twice the rate of men for almost 25 years. They are in all industries, including industries often considered "nontraditional" for women, such as construction, engineering, and wholesale distribution. While your children are young, you may wish to have a small business focused on consulting in your field of expertise. This gives you an opportunity to use your experience, stay up-to-date in the field, and remain visible as a player. This is what Camye Mackey did for several years while her children were small. She then chose to return to the corporate world.

On the other hand, you may wish to build a multimillion-dollar business, as Laura did. Women start businesses because they believe they can deliver a better product or service than their current employer provides, or because they see the need for a product or service that is not being provided. Women's leadership styles stand them in good stead when they make the transition to entrepreneurship. Their skills at relationship building and problem solving are critical to entrepreneurship. Most of the knowledge and tools presented in this book apply to entrepreneurial endeavors as much as to corporate environments.

Options and Opportunities: In Summary

- Seek out lattice assignments.
- Transform your organization.
- Take on turnaround projects.
- Become an intrapreneur.
- Become an entrepreneur.

Continue the Journey

Know When It Is Time to Leave

Making the decision to move on is one of the toughest decisions you have to make. Be certain it is a strategic professional or personal decision.

Senior women leaders rank leaving a company that has given them opportunities to grow and advance for a better position at a different company as one of the most difficult decisions they have faced in their career. Although it is not easy, moving to a new company may be the logical next step in achieving your professional and personal goals. If you have accomplished or learned all you can in your current company, you should be seeking new opportunities and challenges elsewhere.

When you are considering moving to another company, don't forget to consider both the position and the company's culture and values. If it is the right next step for you, make the change. Do not stay at a company out of blind loyalty just because it has been good to you.

Women are more likely to be successful when making a move than men, according to a new study from the Harvard Business School. The very things that distinguish women's leadership styles make the difference. Women are more likely to take into account the culture, values, and management style of the new company and determine if it is a good fit. In addition, women bring with them the strength of their external networks of relationships with clients and outside contacts.[12] When considering a move to a new employer, take the time to do as thorough an investigation as when you chose your first employer. Remember, it is the fit of the company with your values that is the most important factor.

Never leave a company precipitously in a moment of anger or frustration. If the work situation becomes onerous, and you believe you cannot change the situation or it is not worth it to you to correct it, it may well be time to leave. But do it on your terms and in your time. Focus on what is best for advancing your career; consider the options, make your plans, and be the one who controls the situation.

Take into consideration your company's policies when planning to submit your resignation and the responsibility you have for making an effective transition. The more senior you are, the more important it is to work with the company leaders to develop a communications strategy and transition plan for your departure. In particular, focus on what is needed to make the customer feel comfortable. This will be important for your reputation within your industry and future relationships, if appropriate, with customer leaders.

If it is your company's policy to ask people to leave immediately upon submitting a resignation, be prepared to pack up and leave quickly. If the company normally encourages leaders to stay on to assist in the transition, however, consider how much time you will need to effectively transfer your responsibilities.

Always Create Options for the Future

There are other reasons to move on. It may be that the company is not what you thought it was when you joined, or it may be that due to restructuring or mergers, the company no longer offers the opportunities you seek. Whatever the reason, always have in place options for your future.

When Pfizer went through a restructuring, Debra Hanna's position was eliminated. Although she had an internal offer, it was not consistent with either her professional or personal goals. Against the potential for such a situation, she had built her networks both inside and outside the company. "I was in a position to explore both internal and external options. I had realized for a couple of years that I was going to want to move to another area in Pfizer or outside and had been positioning myself for either option. So I had lots of options to consider. I ultimately chose to move to the Critical Path Institute for strategic professional reasons as well as personal reasons."

You may also choose to move on for reasons unrelated to the company; as you move through your career, your professional or personal goals may change. Keep your options open by staying up-to-date in both your industry and the business world in general. Be visible in your industry and in your community so that if the time comes when you want to explore opportunities, you already have the connections to do so.

Continue the Journey: In Summary

- Know when it is time to leave.
- Always create options for the future.

Advocate Unabashedly for Yourself

Advocating for yourself requires an intimate knowledge of your goals, talents, and value to the business. Success Strategy Four takes you through the process of building your personal brand; creating a convincing business case to position yourself as the candidate of choice for opportunities, recognition, or compensation increases; and creating a powerful network of sponsors, mentors, and colleagues who will be the wind beneath your wings throughout your career.

Be Your Strongest Advocate

To achieve your goals, you have to take ownership of your career. You must develop your personal business strategy, showcase your strengths, promote your accomplishments and contributions to the business, quantify the value you bring to the business, and strongly advocate for promotions and compensation increases. The most successful women say these are things they wish they had known earlier in their careers.

"We have to realize the value we, as women, bring to the table and have the courage to stand up for ourselves," says Camye Mackey. "We must showcase our strengths and quantify our contributions."

Maximize Your Personal Brand

A personal brand is your unique selling proposition that differentiates you from everyone else. The same imperatives that underlie branding a company or a product apply to building your personal brand. Having a strong, clear personal brand is critical to your success.

Even if you have not intentionally created a personal brand, by default, you have a brand that other people see. Everything you do, the way you do it, and how you present yourself communicates a brand to others. Instead of leaving your brand to chance, be proactive in taking control of your brand; consciously decide on your personal value proposition and determine how you will present that value. Once you have a well-thought-out brand, you always have clear, consistent talking points about yourself, whether you are meeting new executives, networking, or interviewing for a new position.

Develop a Brand That Is Uniquely Yours

Your brand builds on your definition of success, vision, values, and goals. It reflects your confidence and belief in who you are, and it portrays the added value you bring to every situation. Your brand goes beyond your current job or company. It is who you are wherever you go and whatever you do. It defines what you stand for, regardless of the situation, and it is the foundation for where you are going and what you want to be in the future.

"You have to understand the qualities you want others to see in you to build a professional brand," says Debra Hanna. "Your brand is something that only you can own; only you can develop. From day one, start building your brand and nurture it continuously."

"Don't try to copy other people," says Kim Roberts. "You go in and you do it your way. You won't regret that. What you regret is copying something that you didn't feel was you."

Think of Yourself as a Valuable Asset

Creating a personal brand, as we said earlier, involves the same process as creating a brand for a service or a product; the same imperatives underlie both. Think of yourself as a highly valuable asset.

Nina McLemore is sought-after as a speaker on creating a brand and an image for individuals and their companies. Building a personal brand, according to Nina, consists of the following five key elements:

1. *Brands are built on substance plus form.* Your brand must be built on your competencies and expertise. Begin by defining your current core competencies and what additional competencies you need in order to achieve your goals. Your core competencies should reflect your past successes and stem from your expertise, connections, talents, education, skills, and aspirations for your future.

For example, Nina says her core competencies are firmly rooted in four areas: experience, focus, disposition, and reputation. Here is how she describes herself. She has a reputation for founding and building successful businesses; she is a player. Her brand presents her as a leader with vision, organizational and strategic planning skills, taste and design aesthetics, and financial acumen who focuses on product integrity. Her disposition turns on hard work, persistence, drive, and teamwork. Her reputation brings with it powerful and diverse connections, enabling her to get things done through networks.

Brands reflect performance that lasts. Consistent action, not rhetoric, creates the lasting impression and validates your brand. Your brand reflects your whole package, in every situation and in every action, through:

- Your job performance
- The way you present yourself in speaking, in writing, on the telephone, and in e-mail
- The way you carry yourself
- The way you dress

All too often, women dismiss e-mail or telephone calls as inconsequential—focusing on a quick message and not taking the time to check spelling or the clarity of a message. These seemingly minor lapses in branding carry a disproportionate weight in creating or destroying your image. Your brand will be impacted by every action, and often the smallest ones have the greatest impact.

2. Brands reinforce credibility and integrity. Be honest about who you are and what you can do. It is dangerous to create a brand based on what you think you should be or you wish you were. You will live this brand every day, and the stress of pretending to be something you are not will quickly wear you down. The most successful women leaders are authentic. Authentic leaders recognize and own their strengths and build on them. They are clear about their values and act upon them.

3. Brands provide competitive differentiation. Focus on what differentiates you from everyone else and makes you stand out. No one is looking for a generalist. Identify your areas of expertise, hone in on them, and make them part of your brand.

4. Brands communicate innovation. Take risks on the job, with your career, and in your personal life. Watch for the signals of new trends emerging in your industry, markets, or technology, and be the first to understand them and gain expertise in applying them. Make sure your core competencies are broad enough and that you continually develop new competencies to compete in a world that is changing, chaotic, and uncertain, and that rewards innovation and the first movers.

5. Brands are visual. Whether one-on-one, in a meeting, or giving a speech, first impressions are based almost totally on the visual—how you look, how you present yourself, your body language, your mannerisms, and how you are dressed. People make instant judgments about your intelligence, effectiveness, credibility, and power. Research shows that these first impressions are created within 30 seconds. Because human beings are not comfortable with psychological dissonance, these initial impressions are difficult to reverse. Nina says that according to research, your appearance counts for over half (55 percent) of that first impression; how you speak—tone, inflection, confidence—accounts for 38 percent of the initial impression. In other words, 93 percent of the first impression is driven by how you look and sound. Content—what you say—accounts for a measly 7 percent of that initial impression.

Create an Executive Presence

Nina McLemore says that as a young executive sitting in the back of a room of men who were company presidents, she realized, "the only reason I was in the back of the room and not at the table was that I looked different, that the men in their well-tailored suits and the right shirt and tie looked the part, and I, as a woman didn't. To be successful, you have to create an executive presence—one that says you are successful, smart, assertive, in control and one that is right for the industry or situation."

An executive presence is driven by your overall appearance, clothing, style, personal grooming, and message. Nina says you need to dress, walk, and talk so you take charge when you enter a room. Remember, 55 percent of the first impression is your appearance. What image are you presenting? Nina advises you to start with your clothing, accessories, and grooming. Know what the appropriate style and dress is for the situation. She contends that this is a much more significant challenge for women than for men. There are no clear "uniforms" or style models for women, and there are many more factors to consider: hair, makeup, clothing, jewelry, accessories, and shoes. She recommends investing in the best quality clothing you can afford. It shows, and men, especially senior executives, notice and recognize quality. Make sure everything fits properly, not too tight but never baggy. The balance between too "sexy" and too "dowdy" can be difficult. Nina says when women dress with overt sexuality, the men won't hear them, as their concentration is not likely to be on business, and the other women won't like them. If you are too dowdy, the men won't hear you either, Nina continues. The right image demands a style with confidence, power, and femininity. It includes a good haircut, at least a little make-up, and simple jewelry. It is attractive and feminine without overt sexuality.

"Present yourself with confidence and poise," says Nina. Remember, the way you present yourself accounts for 38 percent of how you are perceived by others. When meeting people, make the first move with a firm handshake, and establish eye contact and a friendly demeanor. Be the first to greet people as they come into your office or to a meeting. Establish connections quickly and easily. Make every individual—whether you are meeting for the first time or reconnecting at work or in a meeting—feel as if she or he is the most important person in the room at that moment by giving the person your entire focus and attention. Ask people questions to understand their positions and make them feel valued. Lean forward in conversation and make eye contact. Lower your pitch and speak with energy and conviction. This conveys credibility and expertise. If you are dealing with people from other cultures, be sure you understand appropriate behaviors and adjust your style accordingly.

When you have set the stage for your message, your audience is primed to receive it. People are ready to hear what you have to say, recommend, or request. Build on your presence to deliver a powerful message with impact.

Nina McLemore concludes, "My appearance has to command authority. You have to establish who you are the minute you walk into a room. That allows others, especially the men, to take my advice, which is often hard advice, and to respect that advice."

Build Your Reputation Strategically

Squash that little voice inside you that says you should be modest about your capabilities, never brag about your accomplishments or awards, and demur when asked to comment off the cuff. Professional self-promotion is not bragging (although many women should do a little more bragging than they do); it is showcasing your capabilities and expertise.

Become sought-after as a speaker. Develop your speaking skills. Many companies offer media and speaking training for managers. The associations you belong to also are likely to have seminars on becoming a powerful speaker who commands attention. Invest in training to build your skills and become a powerful speaker. Develop a few core speeches:

- Your industry overview speech
- Your motivational speech for young professionals
- Your overview of today's business strategies to address emerging challenges

Seek out opportunities to speak both within your company and within your industry to business groups and to women's groups. Be strategic in your selection of speaking venues. At first, you may want to speak at low-profile events to gain experience in speaking and in handling audience questions. As you build your reputation as a speaker, you will begin to receive invitations. Be strategic in selecting events consistent with your brand, goals, and interests.

You may also begin to get invitations to participate on panels. These are excellent opportunities to gain visibility without the preparation required for a speech. They also can be great networking opportunities. Sharon says some of the best contacts she has made have been fellow panelists.

Use publications and awards to enhance your credibility. Write articles or a regular column for industry publications or blogs. The magazines, newsletters, and websites of organizations you support provide excellent publication opportunities. The beauty of being published is that you can send copies of your articles to others—to share information and to generate visibility. Not only will you gain credibility for yourself, you will get credit for promoting the company. Publishing will enhance your reputation within your organization and with your clients.

You are likely to receive awards as you climb the corporate ladder or become visible in volunteer activities. Awards are a strong vehicle for gaining visibility and credibility. Don't wait for someone to nominate you; strategically seek out important, high-profile awards. Work to become nominated and to get these awards.

Make certain your manager and colleagues know about your speeches, publications, and awards. You might forward invitations and invite them to the event where you are speaking or getting an award. If you are concerned about seeming too self-promotional, include a message saying how thrilled you are to be speaking or getting this award and that it would mean so much to you to have them attend. After the event, drop off the program at your manager's office or forward a news clipping covering the event and mentioning you.

Benefit from your company's public relations experts. Public relations departments are always on the lookout for opportunities to publicize the achievements of company employees, so they may send out a press release when you get an award or give an important speech—increasing your visibility. These days, many public relations departments are especially interested in publicizing the achievements of strong women leaders from their company, so they can become your partner in gaining visibility and credibility. When women leaders do interviews, publish, or receive awards, most companies view this as an opportunity to gain positive publicity for the company and to demonstrate its support for women in leadership.

The company may also have public relations policies about speaking, media interviews, or publishing, so be sure to check them out. The public relations professionals can be very helpful in making you more effective and in avoiding bad exposure or negative publicity. Take advantage of the public relations department's expertise. In addition, they can become the follow-up contact for reporters for questions, fact checking, and photos. This minimizes the time you need to devote to these follow-up details.

Human resources departments also are often interested in

publicizing the activities and success of women leaders from your company as they do recruiting. The work of the public relations and human resources departments contribute to the credibility of your personal brand and make it come alive.

Build Your Personal Business Case

A compelling brand is your foundation. Your personal business case makes the argument for you as an asset to the business. A recent Catalyst study reported that the women who were the most proactive in making their achievements visible advanced further and had higher growth. In addition, as a result, they attracted higher-level mentors and sponsors.[1]

You have to take a leadership role in making certain you are being recognized for your successes. Sharon Allen, former Chairman of the Board of Deloitte LLP, says, "I know what a difference the organization can make because Deloitte was really a trailblazer with our women's initiative. But," she continues, "no matter what your organization may do to help you promote your career, at the end of the day, it won't matter unless you perform and watch out for your own career." It is up to you to plan your own career, seize the opportunities, and be willing to promote your own accomplishments.[2]

Build the Case for Promotion or Compensation Increase

Whenever you are seeking a salary increase, a promotion, or a special assignment, you must build a targeted business case to support your request. The fact that you did an outstanding job and met every goal you were asked to achieve and therefore should be rewarded is not sufficient. The women we talked to all focused on the importance of quantifying the value of your past and future accomplishments to the overall success of the business as the foundation for your request.

Track and Quantify Your Successes—Big and Small

You have to be good at making sure everyone knows the positive things you are doing. Keep track of your successes, not just the big ones, but also the daily activities. Be strategic in making your successes visible to your manager and to other executives. Again, it is not about how hard you worked, but about the quantifiable impact your work had on the strategic goals of your business unit and the company. Do this both formally, in performance reviews or progress reports, and informally, in conversation or by sharing accolades you have received.

Early in her career, Beverly Holmes figured out that it was her responsibility to make certain her achievements were recognized. Throughout the year, she kept a diary of her achievements and the problems she resolved. She used the information to create an annual profile of her accomplishments, detailing how those accomplishments contributed to the company's bottom line. She was also very persistent and consistent about addressing her own leadership development opportunities, and took note of what she had learned during the year to improve her performance and output.

Prior to meeting with her manager for her annual review, she would provide him with her portfolio of accomplishments along with her leadership and business development objectives for the coming year. She would also outline what help she needed from her manager to accomplish the agreed-upon goals. "I always felt it was important to engage my manager. Encouraging and receiving his input allowed me to understand what was important to him and the company."

Quantify your accomplishments in every possible way:

- How many new clients you brought to the company
- How much revenue you created for the company from old and new customers and how this contributed to profit
- How you improved a process that saved the company money and increased customer and staff satisfaction

You must be proactive and confident in relating your accomplishments to your manager's objectives, the division results, and the highest-level business outcomes. Show how you contributed to these outcomes. Come right out and say, "I increased throughput by X% in the last three months, which increases your overall business

82

unit's performance by Y%, and contributes to the division's quarterly goals by Z%. "This will not be viewed as boasting, as some women fear; it is simply reporting the facts showing cause and effect. This isn't bragging. This is good business. It all goes back to setting high goals, executing and achieving those goals, and showing you are able to drive results," says Camye Mackey.

Do Your Research

When you are seeking an increase in compensation, study how compensation in your company ties into business results. Diahann Lassus, president and chief investment officer at Lassus Wherley and one of *Worth* magazine's top financial advisors, says, "the biggest challenge many women have is they don't recognize their real value and understate it to the company." She urges women to do their homework prior to discussing compensation and to get professional assistance. "You need to understand the possibilities in terms of compensation and know what you should ask for," adds Diahann.

As you move up the ranks, compensation becomes more complex, and it becomes more difficult to know all the possibilities as well as to understand how your compensation plan at work affects your personal wealth-building strategies. Rather than trying to figure out the possibilities yourself, take advantage of outside help, such as lawyers and financial advisors who specialize in compensation in your industry.

Do the research to see what your job is worth in your company, your industry, and your community. Your professional and industry associations can be an excellent resource. Understand what kind of company you work for and how it structures compensation. In those companies where salary ranges are available, review the ranges for your area and your level of performance. Tie this to your results and your contribution to your department or business unit, your division, and the overall company results. Quantify your contribution to the success of your function, your division, and the overall company results. Relate your accomplishments to your manager's goals. Be specific. "I have increased revenue by this amount." "This is the value of my accomplishments to the business this past year." Equally as important, project your future contribution. "Here is what I project I will bring in next year." "Here is how I will improve this function's performance next year."

Only when you have laid this groundwork are you ready to ask for the compensation package you want. "When you present your results, it makes it easier for your manager to say 'yes,'" says Camye Mackey.

Take a similar approach when asking for a promotion, a new assignment, or a training opportunity. Some experts suggest creating a spreadsheet for yourself to use as a working document when you develop your personal business case. Lay out your accomplishments, and quantify them in terms of contribution to business outcomes. Quantify the benefits of putting you rather than anyone else in the position. What unique qualities do you bring to the job that will substantially increase the outcomes? Be able to answer the question, "If you were to get the position, what would you do differently?" Then close with a strong statement of how you will make a difference to the function and the company. By the time you make your request, it should seem not like a reward but the logical conclusion to the future success of the function and the company.

Ask for What You Want

You can be successful asking for anything if you follow these five steps we have adapted from business strategy coach Mary Cantando.

1. *Know what you want and be very specific about it.* If you are asking for an increase in compensation, know exactly how much you want and how you want the compensation structured. Know the details and lay them out in writing. Be sure your outcome and comparison data are fully documented. If you are asking for a promotion, know what job you want and why having you in the position will benefit the company. Present your request in terms of the benefits to your manager, your business unit, and the company. Picture the end result in your mind.

2. *Write down the exact outcome you want—be specific and focused.* Figure out exactly how you will make the case so the only logical business conclusion is giving you what you want.

3. *Write the request in the form of a call to action.* Engage your manager to support your request and be your advocate. "How can I help you be my advocate for this promotion?"

4. *Practice making the case and asking out loud.* In your mind, think through the entire meeting from the time you enter the office—how you will present your business case and how you will close. Be respectful and not confrontational. Anticipate questions and objections, and prepare your responses. Then repeat your request out loud until you can say it firmly and with conviction.

5. *Expect the answer to be "yes."* Present your case with confidence and enthusiasm. You should be excited about what you have brought to the company and the contributions you expect to make in the future. You are not there as a supplicant. You have earned everything you are requesting. Stick to the script you have laid out, and expect a positive outcome.

No one will advocate for you better than you when you believe in yourself and your capabilities. Present yourself with confidence and pride.

Be Your Strongest Advocate: In Summary

- Maximize your personal brand.
  - Develop a brand that is uniquely yours.
  - Think of yourself as a valuable asset.
  - Create an executive presence.
  - Build your reputation strategically.
- Build your personal business case.
- Build the case for a promotion or compensation increase.
  - Track and quantify your successes—big and small.

- Do your research.
- Ask for what you want.

Create Networks of Advocates and Allies

Building your personal and professional life is not a solo performance. You don't have to do it alone—in fact, you can't. "Reputation is built on both performance and who knows you," says Nina McLemore. The higher up you go in your profession and your company, the more influential who you know and who knows you becomes. One or more well-placed sponsors is the key differentiating factor that determines whether you or someone else will be offered a top position in your company, invited to take a board of directors position, or placed on the short list for a prestigious new position.

Build Multiple Networks

From the start of your career, being active in professional and industry organizations is critical. Research shows that the most successful businesswomen join more organizations than other women and have a more diverse set of networks. They join professional, industry, and community organizations both to learn and to gain visibility and personal networks for support and fellowship.[3] "Building multiple support networks is critical from both a personal and a work perspective," says Maria Coyne.

One of women's strengths is building networks where the members support each other. Men tend to make contacts; women build relationships. Women reach out to others to share information and make introductions. They ask, "*How* are you doing?" as well as, "*What* are you doing?" This strengthens your connections with men as well as with women. Men say they appreciate this extra bit of concern from the women in their networks.

You need networks and relationships inside your company and externally in your industry and profession, as well as general business networks. Networks are vital sources of information and essential as sources of mentors and sponsors. You need different organizations and different mentors for different purposes.

Build Internal Networks of Business Relationships
Building business networks across the entire company helps you understand the goals of the company and make the connections necessary to build your career. Your internal networks should include mentors from across the business spectrum.

Building relationships that help you get things done through working with others is essential to your success. The higher up you go, the more important relationships and the ability to get things done through others become. Support others and they will in turn support you. "Don't dismiss office politics—teach it" blares a headline in the *Wall Street Journal*.[4] The article reports that after five to seven years, your ability to get things done through others becomes a significant part of your role, and by the time you get to senior management, the skill to manage relationships becomes paramount and your technical skills are mostly irrelevant.

"One of the mistakes I see people in the sciences and technical fields make is they only network around their technical expertise," says Debra Hanna. "I started early meeting people in different parts of the business and creating those networks."

In addition to building your own networks, take advantage of existing internal networks. Debra joined Pfizer's Women's Leadership Network and quickly became a cochair and then president of the local networks at a number of sites as she transfered around the company. Through the network, she met women leaders from diverse areas of the business, such as regulation, business strategy, and finance, leaders she would otherwise never have gotten to know. "I met both women and men in senior management through that venue, and that made a huge difference in my trajectory."

Build External Networks of Business Relationships
Join multiple organizations in order to keep up-to-date with your industry and the key players in the industry. This will help you

become knowledgeable about business and related industry issues. It also provides you with the opportunity to be active in areas that align with your values and passions, such as economic development, education, or women's advancement.

From the early days of your career, external networks can create a support system to supplement and complement your work relationships. Networking with other professionals in your field who are experiencing the same challenges as you gives you insight into how others are dealing with these challenges. These are fellow professionals who can share your frustrations, give you practical advice, refer you to experts, and celebrate your successes with you.

The value of building relationships outside your company extends to customers, industry leaders, and business leaders. Use these relationships to learn about trends in the industry, identify new business opportunities, and discover gaps in available products and services that will allow you to create new markets for your company.

"I spend 50 percent of my time with clients," reports Virginia Rometty, the first woman CEO of IBM. "Time is the greatest gift your customers can give you."

Personal connections contribute to your credibility, your reputation, and your visibility with customers, with industry leaders, and colleagues inside your company. They add to your credentials and help make you top of mind when senior positions open up inside your company or in other companies. Nurturing the relationships results in invitations to be part of other networks, to serve on or lead prestigious projects or committees in your industry or your community, and to get introductions to other leaders. These are relationships that you can use to get things done.

Kathe Albrecht became the president of her industry association. "That helped define my career because I became known as someone who knew about the larger issues for the profession and specifically as an expert in copyright law and fair use of museum images." This led to opportunities to become involved in significant projects within the university as well as in her industry.

Building wide-reaching, diverse networks opens up opportunities outside your company. One of Debra Hanna's deliberate networking goals was to have options should she decide to pursue opportunities outside of Pfizer. That time came when her research responsibilities were moved to a group in China, and she was not interested in the internal career opportunities available to her. Coincidently, at the same time, a position focusing on her primary research interests at the Critical Path Institute, a nonprofit health research institute, became available. "Through my network I learned about the position, interviewed very quickly, and found it aligned with my values, my scientific interests, and my desire to be an active player in the global community," says Debra.

Make Networks Work for You
Effective networks are built on give and take. Giving back will increase the value of the network to you. When you join a network and meet new people, look for ways you can contribute both to the group and to each person you meet. Start out by asking what you can do for the other person, whether she or he is a customer, a colleague, or someone you have just met at a conference. Become known as a connector, someone who brings together people who can help each other. Identify opportunities for others they might not know about and make introductions. Invite them to be your guests at a meeting of an organization that might be helpful to them.

Think strategically about your networks. Be crystal clear on which organizations align with your goals and values. Figure out what you want to gain from the organization and what you can give to the group. Invest your time and energy in those organizations that can make a difference in achieving your professional or personal goals. Resist pressure to join organizations that are not meaningful to you.

Be your own best advocate within the organizations. Let others know what you need. Ask for the introductions you want. There is a common saying, "the universe will provide." However, unless you clearly state to the universe—your networks, colleagues, and friends—what it is you want, it will not be able to provide.

Volunteer for organizational leadership positions on the board of directors or leading projects. Taking on leadership positions in your organizations provides a unique opportunity to work closely with, and learn from, some of the most successful executives in your industry and community. Laura says she always sought and accepted opportunities to be on the board of directors or an officer in organizations for this very reason. Taking the initiative to set up one-on-one lunches with the other organizational leaders both benefited her ability to be effective in the organization and allowed her to learn how they ran their larger organizations. They willingly shared their business experience and their company policies, and several became advisors and mentors, providing an education and connections not otherwise available at any cost.

As you review the biographies of the accomplished women who shared their experiences for this book, one of the things that stands out is their involvement beyond their companies in their industry, their communities, and society. As busy as they are, they seek and accept to serve. For example, Monica Luechtefeld helped create the standards for Internet e-commerce in the early days of the Internet and serves as an advisor on Internet and cyber security to the Business Roundtable today. In addition, she is active in women's business groups, the local chamber of commerce, and on the boards of two colleges.

Maria Coyne has served for over a decade on the board of directors of the high school that both she and her daughter attended, and in addition served as chairman for four years. She believes that being involved in the community helps keep her grounded and focused on what's important. Marilyn Johnson's board service includes the Council of Better Business Bureaus, the Asian Pacific Islander American Scholarship Foundation, and the One World Theater in Austin, Texas. Kim Roberts is Chairman of the Board of TractorShare Corporation, a nonprofit organization focused on agricultural empowerment in developing countries.

Adjust Your Networks as Needed

Building networks is an ongoing process. As your job changes, your interests expand, and your personal life evolves, you may need to realign your networks. A change in your position, a move to a different part of the company—for example, from operations to marketing—or a reorganization within your company may require expanding current networks or building new networks both within and outside the company. Don't feel compelled to continue to participate in organizations that no longer align with your interests.

After moving to a new organization, you will want to focus on both internal and external networks related to the new company. When Debra Hanna moved to the Critical Path Institute, she immediately began building not only her internal networks but also new external networks to develop insight into the nonprofit world and to become active in her new community.

As you advance up the career ladder, both your internal and external networks will become more diverse or change to incorporate the new relationships that are important to getting your job done and to your continued advancement. As you become eligible for organizations of senior leaders, seek out those that will give you the knowledge you need and the support to help you deal with the challenges of your new role.

Network Broadly

While one of women's strengths is the quality of the relationships they build, there also is value in becoming widely known. The more ex-colleagues you have who are highly placed or sitting on boards, the more likely you are to be endorsed for board positions and the higher your board compensation will be—on average 6 percent more. Find reasons to stay in touch with leaders who have been in your networks. Keep them posted on your progress, achievements, and interests. Staying on their radar increases the likelihood you will be top of mind when an opening occurs.[5]

Develop and Nurture a Network of Mentors

Everyone needs both mentors and sponsors. While most people are familiar with the concept of mentors, many do not understand the value and role of sponsors. Mentors provide guidance; sponsors are advocates for you. Sometimes a mentor will also function as a sponsor. More often, you will need to cultivate both mentors and sponsors.

Successful businesswomen agree that mentors are invaluable. "I've found mentors extraordinarily important throughout my career," says Monica Luechtefeld. "I try to have at least one or two at any point in time, usually outside my area."

Most successful women have a network of mentors, both inside and outside their company. Internally, mentors can be anywhere in the company. Having internal mentors outside your immediate area is valuable to learn about other functions and areas of the business as well as to become known to leaders across the business. In addition, current or former managers often become mentors.

Expand your network of mentors beyond your company. "You need multiple mentors for multiple reasons," says Maria Coyne. "You have some mentors at work and some outside work who will help you with your professional development and help you fill in gaps." Having mentors with similar and diverse backgrounds will expand your understanding of the challenges and opportunities both in your industry and in other areas.

Maximize the Value of Mentors

A mentor is someone you can go to for advice about a challenging project you have undertaken, how to get over a hurdle, or how to deal with specific issues. Mentors serve as sounding boards, let you know if you are on the right track, and help you think through a situation. Mentors do not give you the solution; they help you think about the range of solutions.

"I can't say enough about having the right mentors," says Debra Hanna. "Having someone other than your boss who knows your strengths to bounce ideas off when you are making stressful decisions and choices, someone who will challenge your thinking, and help you make solid decisions is incredibly valuable."

Mentors also expand your ideas for career advancement and open your eyes to opportunities you never would have known about or considered. They have a different perspective on the business, seeing it from a more senior level, and can identify possibilities and potential that would never have occurred to you. In addition, mentors have a rare view of you and your qualifications, and can identify opportunities for you to capitalize on those qualifications—again opportunities you might never have known about. They can transform the way you think about yourself and your perceptions of what you can achieve and what your career can be. Their insights and advice can move your career goals to new heights.

Laura has a powerful example of how a mentor can transform your perception of yourself. Over lunch one day, one of her mentors asked her if she had thought about becoming Secretary of Health and Human Services (HHS). He told her that the combination of her experience in public policy and the major health issues facing the country made her an excellent candidate for the office. At first, Laura was stunned by the suggestion; however, after reflection, she thought, "Why not?" She actually considered it as an option. Although Laura decided she had no interest in this political appointment, she says his suggestion transformed her perception of herself and made her think very differently about what levels she should consider for her professional goals and possibilities. "He took me from seeing myself as a novice in business to recognizing how I had professionally matured and developed."

One of Sharon's lifelong mentors is the professor who was chair of her dissertation committee. He always saw her potential as higher than she did, and to this day, continues to open her eyes to new possibilities. He gets a little smile on his face when he is about to suggest she undertake something totally unlike anything she has ever done before. He is a sounding board, an enthusiastic supporter, and he has used his professional connections to open doors for her. When she is successful at something he set her up for, he tries to act as if he had no question about her ability to do the job. But, underneath, it is obvious that he takes great pride in her accomplishments, and that is very special.

Ask for Help and Feedback

Sometimes women are reluctant to ask for help or advice. They fear this is tantamount to admitting that they are not competent. Yet, mentors and sponsors say one of the most rewarding parts of being an advisor is seeing feedback being put into action and making a difference for their mentees. In fact, seeing that you know when to ask for feedback and how well you use that feedback is a primary factor in their evaluation of your leadership strengths. Both mentors and sponsors say that it is important to see that their protégés not only accept feedback, but act upon it.

Never Stop Cultivating Mentors

Mentors are important wherever you are in your career progression, from the early days through senior management. "Throughout my career, I was blessed with people who had the expertise or resources that were important to my success, both personal and professional," says Beverly Holmes. "Some brought specific skills and advice; others were professional or spiritual mentors. But I must say all my encounters whether short or long, positive or negative, had a profound impact on my ability to accomplish my goals and grow as a leader. Without a doubt all their input made me a better person."

Even when Virginia Rometty was ready to become IBM's CEO, she continued to turn to mentors for advice. One of these mentors was Maggie Williams, chief executive of Frontier Communications Corporation. Virginia wanted to know what was important to increasing her effectiveness as an executive and what experiences she needed to prepare her for the new opportunity. Maggie Williams told her that a big part of being a CEO of a public company is to work closely with Wall Street and advised her to start developing relationships with Wall Street leaders, big banks, and key IBM customers she didn't already know.

Different mentors fill different needs. Your mentors may change over time as your needs change.

In a few cases, you will develop a relationship that continues throughout your career. Beverly Holmes recalls a special individual who was a mentor and confidant throughout her career. "When I needed help, I would call. He never turned me away, and he never said, 'This is what you should or should not do.' He always gave me different points of view, and when I left the meeting, I had a sense of the direction I should take. It was always gratifying to me to know that good people are placed into your life for your good. It was an excellent lesson learned and a practice I tried to emulate in my role as a leader and mentor."

Be Selective in Identifying Mentors

Mentorships may evolve as a result of informal or formal contacts. Several women we interviewed reported that leaders reached out to them and became their mentors. But it is most effective to take the initiative to identify the mentors you need and approach them.

Some large companies are introducing formal mentorship programs. However, many women say these programs often result in make-work assignments or task force assignments that add workload without increasing skills, knowledge, or visibility. Mentorships are not the same as professional development programs. Mentorships provide informal advising on an as-needed basis.

Except in those cases where companies have formal mentorship programs, mentorships are not based on a formal agreement. Even if your company has a formal program, supplement it with additional mentors based on your goals and needs.

Be strategic in seeking and selecting mentors. Include both women and men among your mentors. Within the company, look for leaders across diverse business areas of the company. Usha Pillai says she often would set up informal informational meetings with leaders in areas outside her immediate area to learn about other business areas. She says no one ever turned down her request for an informal meeting and many of these conversations resulted in mentorships.

Mine your networks outside the company for mentors who complement and supplement your internal mentor network. Mentorships are not limited to professional interests. Many women have mentors who can be sounding boards when they are dealing with personal or general career issues or with being a woman in leadership. No one mentor can answer all of your questions or advise you on every situation; it is important to have a variety of perspectives.

Help Your Mentor Help You
Figure out what you want from each mentor relationship and let your mentors know. Share your goals with your mentors. Mentorships are as much about dealing with challenges in your current position as about developing networks, learning of new opportunities, or gaining introductions to leaders or networks to help you progress in your career. Make the relationship with your mentors a two-way street—look for ways you can give back to your mentors. It may be as simple as sending your mentors articles or reports of interest to them. If your mentor is in your management chain, look for ways to make her or him look good. Provide input to a project, help with a report or project, or take something off her or his desk and complete the assignment. Most mentors say the best reward is seeing that you are taking their advice seriously and you are succeeding.

Recognize and Accept the Value of Sponsors

A sponsor is someone who is well connected either within your company or in your industry. It is someone who will advocate for you and facilitate your movement into top leadership positions. Sponsors provide stretch opportunities, form critical connections, and promote your visibility. A recent study from the Center for Work-Life Policy published in the *Harvard Business Review* characterizes sponsorship as the "last glass ceiling." Women are much less likely than men to have highly placed political allies to propel them forward, inspire them, and protect them through the "perilous straits of upper management."[6] Performance does count; but who knows about you and has confidence in your capabilities is critical.

Women underestimate the importance of sponsors. The Center for Work-Life Policy study found sponsorship accounts for up to 30 percent in getting more stretch assignments, promotions, and pay raises.[7] Yet, more than three-quarters of women still believe that hard work alone will result in organizational advancement.

Equally as worrisome is that even those who recognize the role of sponsors often are uncomfortable with cultivating sponsorship relationships and having sponsors advocate for them. Many women believe that they should advance and be offered senior positions based on merit alone, and that there is something unsavory about cultivating sponsor relationships.[8] One woman we know left her company when she reached middle management specifically after realizing that continued advancement was based as much on developing sponsors and personal connections as it was based on performance—she believed this was unfair and wrong.

While women are uncomfortable with the concept of others advocating for them, they often are persuasive and passionate champions for others. Think about the last time you had a position to fill. What did you do? Whatever the company procedures for posting jobs, you still turned to colleagues you trust and asked if they had any recommendations. The more critical the job is, the more weight you place on hiring someone who is a known quantity to a colleague you trust. It is no different at the highest levels of the business.

The most successful businesswomen have learned to overcome their reluctance to advocate for themselves and to cultivate sponsors who will advocate for them. They recognize that top leaders turn to their trusted advisors when openings occur. Even more than at the lower levels, the endorsement of one or more highly placed colleagues carries a great deal of weight. Despite publicized formal searches, most CEO and board positions in the United States are filled through personal referrals.

Sponsorships Benefit Sponsors as Well as You
There are rewards for the sponsor as well as for the person being sponsored. Recognize that part of a senior executive's reputation is

his or her ability to bring top talent to the table and for the candidates he or she sponsors to be star performers. There is a definite advantage for sponsors from advocating for top-notch people. Identifying top talent adds to their reputation and career recognition. By putting yourself on their radar, you are giving them the opportunity to champion a high performer. Perhaps the best selling point is that sponsors view being a sponsor as part of their legacy. Both women and men sponsors say the most important benefit to them of being a sponsor is the satisfaction in "paying it forward."[9]

Create and Maintain Your Network of Sponsors

As with mentors, you need to take the initiative to build a network of multiple sponsors in different areas within the company and outside the company. Having advocates looking out for you in multiple arenas protects you from being at the mercy of changes in leadership or a given sponsor leaving the company. As you move up the hierarchy, as the business changes, or as your goals change, you will need to continue to adjust your sponsor network to reflect your new situation. Your network of sponsors should be strategic, not only positioning you for the current job, but positioning you for your long-range career growth.

The more sponsors you have, the better. Having multiple endorsements when you are being considered for an opportunity reenforces and strengthens the recommendation. Develop and cultivate a broad and diverse network of sponsors.

Know What You Want

As with mentors, you need to help your sponsors help you. You must be very clear about your goals and what you want before you can ask someone else to help you. Share your goals and interests with those who can be sponsors for you; make certain they know about your accomplishments and why you are an excellent candidate for senior-level and board positions. Keep your sponsors updated on your successes and interests. Do not wait for a specific opportunity to become available to start preparing the groundwork. By the time opportunities become public knowledge, the selection is all but complete. You want to be certain that when a senior executive is asked for a recommendation, you are top of mind.

Manage the Unmentionables

One of the challenges identified in the Center for Work-Life Policy study was men's reluctance to give guidance to women on how to adjust their style, clothing, and executive presence to look the part of a leader. This is feedback they easily and frequently give to men.[10] Make it easy for them. Find an appropriate opportunity to ask for feedback on your style or executive presence. Try a different style and then ask if they have seen a difference.

This is a good reason to include women as sponsors. Identify senior women and observe their style. Set up an informal meeting or invite some of the senior women you know for coffee, and ask for their advice. We know executive presence is an important component in being viewed as having executive potential. Don't ignore it; figure out how to create a comfortable situation to get the feedback you need.

Another challenge is the unspoken concern that the relationship between an older, more powerful man and a younger woman will create speculation of an affair.[11] While it is unlikely such speculation will ever totally disappear, there are ways of handling it. First and foremost, don't! From the beginning of your career, do not be drawn in by the attraction of an affair, whether with a senior executive, a manager, a colleague, or someone who works for you. At the same time, don't avoid dinners, meetings, or travel with men because you fear the potential for gossip. Just always act appropriately and in a businesslike manner.

The best defense, however, is performance. If others can see that you earned your promotions and opportunities, there is less likely to be speculation about an affair. Your performance allows your supporters to squash rumors of inappropriate behavior. Your team may well become your best champions. Sharon learned some years after the fact that one of her male employees was her best defender against rumors of inappropriate behavior. When he joined his male colleagues for drinks after work, he later told Sharon, they often engaged in speculation about her relations with senior executives. He was offended by the gossip because he felt it detracted from the very high accomplishments of the team, so whenever the topic came up, he was proactive in addressing it by pointing out Sharon's achievements.

Nurture the Sponsor Relationship
Developing a sponsor relationship is more delicate than recruiting a mentor. Look for ways to gain visibility and get to know potential sponsors through special assignments, making presentations at program reviews, or attending meetings. Make a point of introducing yourself to potential sponsors at company meetings or formal social events such as client dinners or company outings.

While mentors may come and go over time, sponsor relationships tend to be longer term. Sponsors need to be confident that you are a top performer and have the potential to be successful in a higher-level position. The sponsor's reputation depends on your being able to perform. A sponsor may be someone you work with directly or someone who has the opportunity to observe your performance over time. In many cases, the sponsor relationship may be more directed than with a mentor and often involves one-on-one meetings where the sponsor may provide specific feedback on performance and advice on how to handle challenging situations.

As with all networking, sponsorship is a two-way street. If your sponsor is also your boss, take work off her or his desk, go the extra mile on a project, or cover for her or him when backup is needed. Find ways to make your sponsor look good as well as showcase your abilities.

Create Networks of Advocates and Allies: In Summary

- Build multiple networks.
  - Build internal networks of business relationships.

- Build external networks of business relationships.
- Make networks work for you.
- Adjust your networks as needed.
- Network broadly.
- Develop and nurture a network of mentors.
  - Maximize the value of mentors.
  - Ask for help and feedback.
  - Never stop cultivating mentors.
  - Be selective in identifying mentors.
  - Help your mentor help you.
- Recognize and accept the value of sponsors.
  - Sponsorships benefit sponsors as well as you
  - Create and maintain your network of sponsors.
  - Know what you want.
  - Manage the unmentionables.
  - Nurture the sponsor relationship.

Translate the Stories Numbers Tell to Drive Strategic Results

In Success Strategy Three, "Be the Architect of Your Career," we talked about two factors that are critical to advancing in business: focusing on outcomes and results, and getting profit-and-loss experience. To be effective in these two areas, you must understand the financial fundamentals of your company, how it makes money, what management's financial philosophy is, and how this translates into action in the decisions you make for your business unit or department.

Being able to tie your actions to the overall results of the business makes you act differently when making decisions. You will be more effective in presenting your results to management when you can frame them in terms of their contribution to the entire business. You will be more successful in advocating for new projects or for your personal advancement. Most of all, when you understand the business of the business, you will be more confident in your job and more likely to be considered as leadership material.

When we asked the women we interviewed what they wished they had done differently in their careers, most said they wished they had taken more business courses and had taken those courses early in their career. Their advice to women starting out: "Get a sound foundation in business."

In this chapter we first discuss how to overcome any trepidation you might feel about your foundation in finance and your ability to translate what the numbers show into meaningful action. Then the chapter takes you through the most critical financial measurements and shows what these measurements can tell you about the culture of the company, how the business operates, and what has an impact on success. We will discuss these critical financial measurements from the perspective of the entire company. Understand that you must take each of these financial measurements and apply them to your own department or business unit. Think of your business unit as a microcosm of the entire business.

Once you know what affects the enterprise's bottom line on a macro level, you can understand the results you have to deliver at your level to contribute to its success. This should affect how you establish your budgets, what you track and measure in your operations, how you make decisions about projects, and where you focus plans for expansion. Use your understanding of your company's overall financial philosophy to structure proposals for new projects, products, or services. Tailor your business cases to reflect the financial priorities of your company and its tolerance for risk.

Laura's Story

I remember the exhilarating, frightening first days of starting my company. I had been a vice president of a company that provided support to the health agencies of the federal government of the United States. With the blessing of that company, I took my 15 staff members and the three months of work remaining on our contracts and launched my company, Prospect Associates—hoping my prospects would be as good as my entrepreneurial dreams and would somehow avoid the pitfalls of the nightmares that consistently woke me at 2:00 a.m.

It was abundantly clear to me that I wanted to build a financially well-run company so I could make payroll for those 15 colleagues who took the risk of coming to work for me, and, in the end, I wanted this company to build the "wealth" I would need to support my handicapped father and sister, as well as the rest of my family, in the years to come. And, to be honest, I wanted to show those folks who had not taken me seriously that they had been wrong.

For me, success was not limited to financial aspirations. I wanted to build a company known for quality and innovation, to be the employer of choice for the best and the brightest, and to be seen as a "Parkway Patriot" instead of a "Beltway Bandit" (the term used pejoratively to describe an unscrupulous government contractor).

My dream was for my employees to not have to face barriers based on gender, race, sexual orientation, religion, or anything other than professional capabilities. I wanted to create an environment where it was possible for employees to achieve economic independence and avoid traps like having to stay in a relationship because of financial dependence. Many women in 1979 believed the only route to financial independence or security was through a husband. Like many women my age, as a child, I was taught that my career choices were being a teacher, a nurse, or a secretary. The pink-collar world was very restrictive and did not offer salaries sufficient to buy a home or create an adequate retirement fund. I knew I wanted something else for my colleagues and for me.

From the very beginning, I knew I wanted Prospect Associates to grow and develop value sufficient for me to live well. I didn't know what that meant in terms of dollars, but I knew what it meant in terms of security and quality of life. Having grown up poor, I wanted and needed financial security. I also wanted to have sufficient money to enjoy life and the opportunities it brought to my loved ones and me. I wanted to educate my children through graduate school so they would not start their lives with high levels of debt.

I wanted to have sufficient money to contribute to causes that were important to me. And I wanted to be able to do all of the things I had dreamed about in my life: travel, own a house with a cutting-edge kitchen, and have someone clean my house once a week. While at the time I probably did not recognize all this as wanting to create wealth, now I know it was all about having the financial resources I needed to live the life I wanted.

Women are often uncomfortable admitting to others that they want to build wealth, but each of us needs to accept that it is financially necessary to create the wealth necessary to build a comfortable life for ourselves and for our families. Recognizing this reinforced my need to gain the expertise to effectively run the business aspects of Prospect Associates.

While numbers and business finances were interesting to me, I knew I needed to learn the business of the business I was starting, and I needed to learn it fast. In my usual strategy of quick learning, I began inviting colleagues to lunch: accountants, bankers, CEOs, anyone who could teach me about finance. I asked each to tell me what he or she thought I needed to know. Interestingly, nobody told me I needed to be good at numbers; rather, they all told me what was important was to understand "the stories that the numbers told."

No one said no to my invitation. In fact, most even paid for lunch! It is always amazing how generous people are with their time and advice. With some exceptions, the more successful people are, the more generous they are in helping folks on their way up. I learned three important lessons from these lunches:

- First, the job of management is to ensure that the company is healthy in all ways—financially, technically, politically, and culturally.
- Second, I knew I would have to work hard and pledge my home as collateral for my $250,000 line of credit.
- Third, it was smart to feel it was appropriate to build wealth for myself and my family.

From this process, I gained an entirely new way of looking at business, talking about business, and taking judicious business risks. I moved from feeling inadequate in the financial aspects of the company to finding that the business of the business was a lot of fun. Figuring out how I could maximize profits and minimize expenses was like a chess game. I loved figuring out strategies for our projects and ways to deliver our services that would provide the outcomes customers wanted with a budget that would give us a competitive edge. Part of the fun was identifying how we could turn financial risks into opportunities. I also began to see how differently I was treated by clients, colleagues, and advisors because I had mastered the language of business. It was like I had been accepted into the club.

Make Business Acumen a High Priority

Business acumen is having the knowledge and skills to understand the business fundamentals of your company, the ability to decipher complex and uncertain situations and their financial implications for your company, and the decisiveness to take appropriate actions that will effectively respond to challenges while enhancing your company's financial performance.

The higher you are in management, the more important business acumen, especially financial sophistication, becomes. By the time you are ready to make the move into senior leadership, it is absolutely critical. Some attribute the slowdown in women's advancement once they reach middle management to a lack of business acumen. There is no question that women are fully capable of succeeding in financial management. It is a matter of acquiring the knowledge, skills, and experience early in your career. You must make this a top priority.

Business acumen brings together a thorough understanding of your company, the wisdom developed from addressing and solving complex business problems, and the confidence to assertively take advantage of opportunities and respond to risks. When a business opportunity or challenge arises, the best leaders quickly analyze the situation, identify the potential implications for the company and its financial performance, develop the pros and cons of possible strategies, and move with confidence to action.

While some of the skills, such as financial sophistication, can be learned through courses or books, financial acumen is acquired from on-the-job experience and from mentors. Seek out opportunities that will provide the experiences you need to fully develop your business acumen and work with mentors who can provide insights that lead to wisdom.

Commit to Mastering Financial Skills

Numbers tell stories that are important to every person involved in a company's management. Women must be sure they develop financial competency not only to meet the fiscal responsibilities of their jobs, but also because these are necessary life skills. Making wise decisions about your financial security requires understanding both business and personal finances.

Like Laura, many women come into the business world not totally prepared to deal with the financial and operational aspects integral to being a manager. Many have never been encouraged in school to focus on math and science. As a result, they are not confident in their ability to decipher business reports and figure out what the numbers mean. Overcoming this lack of confidence and mastering the skills you need to provide the financial oversight required at senior levels is critical if you are to advance to any leadership or managerial role.

Diahann Lassus says, "So much about women and finance is about the confidence of believing you can do it. And so much of the issues women have about finance are they don't believe they can do it. They don't believe they have that ability. So many of the conversations we have with women around personal financial planning is in the mode of: 'Absolutely, you're smart enough to do this. There's no reason you can't understand.' We just need to take it and frame it in a different way in terms of how you use it as a tool."

You too can master the art of business and have a lot of fun doing it. The necessity of learning about financial management is the same whether you are an entrepreneur like Laura or a manager in a company owned by others. "Regardless of where you are in the organization, you need to act like you are an owner," concludes Maria Coyne.

Combining an understanding of the financial operations of business in general with an intimate knowledge of the financial and operational fundamentals of your business and industry is required for you to be successful as a leader in your company. Ultimately, the actions of a company's management determine its success. "You need to know the business inside and out. That means knowing the financials, the employee and guest needs, as well as the expectations of the owner," says Camye Mackey.

As you go through the process of learning about your company's financial operations, you gain insights into its culture, the opportunities and challenges it faces, and the value of profit and growth. These insights will influence your decision making and provide a strong foundation for interacting with senior management. "I grew really passionate about understanding the business of science," says Debra Hanna. "That is not something they teach you in school."

Many young people in their early career days, especially women, don't believe that understanding the business of business pertains to them. It is critical to learn as early in your career as possible, however, that your company's finances absolutely pertain to you. Everything you do as a technical person or a leader contributes to the success of the business. Understanding the company's financials will give you greater insight into the company, helping you better see opportunities for new products or services or for introducing new strategies to improve operational performance.

"Understanding the impact of your actions on the company's goals gives you and your area a real legitimacy," says Maria Coyne. Further, determining what actions you should take or how to advocate for yourself or your ideas will be easier if you understand the financial and operational implications of varying approaches.

Once you understand the company's financial culture, you can use the outcomes and measurements that you know the company values in your discussions and presentations. The bottom line is that by spending time with people, within and outside your organization, who can help you learn about finance, you will gain insight into how you can do your job better and support your ideas in a manner that will make them consistent with the company's values and strategic direction.

Gain Financial Competency

Usha Pillai said that the challenges in her mind as she began to advance were, "How does a company the size of Pfizer operate? How does it make its decisions? How many pills does it have to sell in a day to be able to support a research function such as the one I am in?" So she specifically targeted people in key positions who could answer her questions; she called, introduced herself, and asked if she could come speak to them to learn about their function. She says no one ever turned her down; she received a world-class education in how the company worked, and ended up being offered a position in global business development by one of the managers she had met informally.

In order to become financially knowledgeable about your company, become a private investigator and learn about your company and its finances. Focus on what questions to ask and learn what comparisons you need to see. Find the people in your organization who truly understand the financial world within your organization and use them as your guides.

Every organization is different. When Debra Hanna moved to a medical research nonprofit institute, she had to learn the finances of business specific to that organization. "I worked very hard in my 90-day transition period to understand what drives the finances of this organization. Obviously what drives a nonprofit organization is different, and I had to learn about funding sources, grants, and philanthropic donations. Understanding that is incredibly important."

Understand the Fundamentals
of Your Company's Finances

Like Usha Pillai and Debra Hanna, take the initiative and time to learn about how your company thinks about, and uses, money. Ask questions like the ones discussed below to begin your journey. The more you learn, the more questions will come to you. You will become curious about how the financial aspects work, and you will begin to better understand what you can do to contribute to the financial health of the organization.

Identify Your Company's Cash Requirements and Sources

Cash is queen. Learn how your company uses cash, where it comes from, and how it affects your day-to-day decisions and goals. The single-largest reason firms get into financial trouble and fail is because they do not have enough cash on hand to meet their current obligations. It is the responsibility of management to be sure there is cash to meet the company's needs. Be sure you understand how cash flow works in your company and how your business unit can affect it.

What is the company's strategy for meeting its day-to-day need for cash? The more successful a company is, the more important it is for the company to have a stable cash source. Many believe growth is mandatory for a company's survival, but growth puts a great stress on cash flow. Imagine that your company is growing, getting more business every month. Is this success? Well, yes, but with growth, each month your company spends more money than it made the month before. What sources of cash does the company have to meet those additional cash needs?

Although each industry has its own standards, management's attitude toward the amount of cash they want to keep on hand differs from company to company. Some companies keep large amounts of cash on hand because they believe it allows them to be nimble, to take advantage of opportunities, and to respond to challenges in a way that keeps them ahead of their competitors. The management of other companies keeps as little cash on hand as possible and invests cash in innovative projects, research, or strategic acquisitions.

Learn what the issues are that affect cash flow. Learning how long it takes your company to be paid by its customers will provide you great insight into cash needs. Reducing the time it takes to get invoices paid will immediately improve the company's profit margin because it will decrease the company's needs for cash. If your customers pay late, your company will have to find the cash to meet its expenses as it waits to be paid. There are costs involved in your company's use of money. For instance, if the company must borrow money to cover expenses until it gets paid, it will incur interest charges. The longer your company needs to wait for payment, the more interest it may have to pay. On the other hand, if your company uses its own cash to cover expenses as it waits to be paid, the company may lose opportunities to use those same dollars for strategic investments.

The impact of economic downturns can dramatically influence the time it takes from sending invoices to receiving payments. As the economy goes through a recessionary period, consumers begin to pay their bills more slowly. From that, a domino effect begins, as companies have less cash on hand to pay their vendors. Internal challenges in times of recession can also affect the level of available cash.

Companies use a broad range of strategies to get their clients to pay faster. For example, in the first years that Laura's company existed, her director of finance hand-carried the company's invoices to the clients. He made sure the person responsible for accounts payable knew the impact slow payment would have on this start-up company—interest rates at that time were above 20 percent. Because of the personal attention, the clients often wrote the checks while her director waited. Laura says this attention to the critical issue of cash flow kept her company in business as its growth rate held at over 60 percent per year for her first five years in business.

If you are working for an entrepreneurial or a midsize business, find out where the company got its start-up capital. Learning what the source of the capital to start up the company was will give you valuable insights into its culture and its attitude toward cash. Was the initial capital from venture capitalists, bank loans, business angels (families and friends), or the entrepreneurs' savings? How aggressive or conservative the owners were at the beginning will give you some idea of the company's attitude toward investments in new opportunities and its tolerance for risk. From this, you gain great insight into how to approach senior management about your requests for investments in your ideas.

How does the company finance large investments like new buildings, research and development, or salary increases? Does the company have access to large amounts of cash, or does it struggle to keep the cash at an adequate level?

What is the company's current cash situation? How many months could the company operate on the cash it has in the bank? You should know what the norms are for this in your industry. You should also know whether your company is cash rich or cash poor, as this will influence managerial decisions at all levels. Understanding this will also give you insight into how your business unit can contribute to your company's well-being. You will find that your contributions to management will have more impact if you are able to discuss issues within the context of the company's current and future cash situation.

Understanding the company's current obligations and its long-term debt will also help you to make better decisions about your budget and day-to-day operations. It may also lead to new ideas for operational approaches and innovation.

Discover How Your Company Makes and Loses Money
It is amazing how few people understand how their company makes money. Leaders of organizations are responsible for the health of their organizations and must understand not only how the company makes money, but also how it can lose money.

Learn how your company makes money. Is it selling a product that requires years of investment in research and development? Does it make money by selling the time of its staff, or is it selling products manufactured in developing countries? There are many models for making money; understanding both the income and expense sides of the equation is a necessity in any management role. Having a solid understanding of all of the elements involved in turning a profit will make you more effective in making decisions about your department or business unit and will help you understand the impact of your decisions on the organization as a whole.

What parts of your company generate income? What parts of your company are expenses? How does your organizational unit influence short-term and long-term profits? What are the implications for your business area of being a staff function that is an expense or a sales organization that generates revenue? While it is imperative to understand in detail all the aspects of the organizational units you oversee, understanding the operational functions and challenges of all company units on a more global basis will increase your effectiveness as a manager.

What is your company's profit margin and how does it compare to the industry? Understanding how the two stack up will show you how your company is truly doing. Understanding the rationale behind your company's position will be invaluable in determining how your company should focus as it moves forward. It will also give you the foundation on which to base your business area's actions so they contribute to the whole organization, and to position new ideas or projects.

What are the ways your company can increase profits and avoid risks in order to remain financially healthy? What roles can your group play to contribute to the company's profitability? Are there actions you and your group can take to reduce losses?

Demonstrating your understanding of the company's finances and the issues affecting its profitability positions you as a viable candidate for senior assignments and advancement. As your responsibilities increase, you will move from managing a single unit within your organization to managing and integrating multiple units. Understanding how these units fit into the whole and play into the financial operations of the company will be mandatory for you to do your job effectively. These skills will give you the ability to see opportunities and challenges beyond the parochial view of your organizational units. Managers who understand the roles and challenges of all company units may also find it easier to work companywide because managers of other groups may feel more comfortable working with them.

Take time to learn about the issues and trends outside your company's control that affect its profitability. Are there, for example, taxes or government regulations affecting your organization's profitability? Are any of these current issues where changes in public policy may affect your company? If so, follow these issues in the news so you understand potential exposures or opportunities that the company should take into consideration. Are there areas within your company that are scrutinized by regulators or by the press? How do these affect the company and the business decisions it is making? These issues can affect the timing for proposing new projects or introducing new products.

Understand the Financial Goals and the
Financial Culture of Your Company
Does your company have a written strategic plan stating its financial goals? If so, does this plan truly drive the company's behavior? Some organizations develop lofty strategic goals and then ignore them in day-to-day decision making. Other companies develop strategic plans and use them as the driving force behind all actions. It is important to understand what management wants to accomplish financially and be sure your decisions and discussions reflect this understanding.

Like individuals, companies have a tolerance for taking advantage of opportunities and accepting financial risk. Historically, how successful has your company been in meeting its financial goals? Understanding your company's financial culture in relation to its financial goals will serve you well as you work to address technical and managerial issues.

Do the company's initiatives, budgets, and projections match the company's strategy? If not, how do they differ and why? How does senior management view financial investments and financial risk taking? Would you describe senior management as conservative risk takers who avoid all but the safest risks, judicious risk takers who weigh the pros and cons of risk taking and proceed based on careful consideration, or high risk takers who may seek high-profit opportunities with inherent high risks as a standard way of doing business? Learning how your management thinks and makes decisions about investments and risks will be very valuable to you as you develop your business area's plans, consider possible proposals for expansion or change, and prepare your annual budget.

How does your company respond to differing economic times? Management's reactions to times of great financial abundance or of economic and business challenges will give you insights into how management thinks about investments and what risks they tolerate.

Understanding what return on investment (ROI) management expects, or what length of time they are comfortable with for moving initiatives from concept to cash, will be helpful in developing your ideas and advocating for the company's investment in them. Understanding what senior management's concerns are will help you develop the elements of your presentations so you can address and allay the concerns up front.

If your company is publicly traded, what are Wall Street's expectations? Wall Street's expectations are extremely strong influencers of decisions within publicly traded companies. Understanding the consequences of these expectations for your group is important. As you reach the company's higher levels, it will be necessary for you to understand the implications of these forces companywide, as your responsibilities may involve your overseeing and integrating the actions of multiple business areas. Being aware of these issues from the beginning of your career and following changes in the strategies will help you adjust your business area's plans and projects.

If your company is not publicly traded, what drives the company's financial strategy? Are either management or the owners working to position the company to go public or to be sold? Do the company owners expect to be paid dividends on a regular basis? If the company is in the process of going public, this will affect what top management expects from business units' goals, plans, and budgets.

All companies have situations that drive their attitude toward financial performance. Understanding what drives your company's actions related to profitability will be invaluable to you as you work in management. It will give you the information you need to make your decisions consistent with the goals of the owners. Having this knowledge will also give you a foundation for developing strategies to meet management's objectives and will enable you to make decisions consistent with the organization's direction.

Know the Financial Decision Makers
Learning who makes the decisions and their level of authorization can assist you in understanding what relationships will be important for

your career advancement. Becoming known to decision makers will become more important as your responsibilities increase. Look for opportunities to work with the decision makers to learn their priorities and make the connections that will hold you in good stead if you are seeking financial advice or support for new initiatives.

Is there consistency in attitude among the company's financial decision makers concerning investment and risk taking? What types of initiatives have each advocated for in the past, and what can you learn about the company from their actions and interests? Are the decision makers optimistic or pessimistic? How much authority do managers at each specific level have? How does this influence your ability to get access to the appropriate funding for new projects?

Create your strategy for developing relationships with the decision makers and gaining credibility for your capabilities. Informal access to senior management will be invaluable to you in understanding how as a team they look at money and think about risk.

Know Your Company's Customers and Competitors

Sitting in a class at Harvard Business School, Laura listened carefully to the answers when the professor asked, "What is the most important element a company must have to survive and be financially successful?" The class—all business owners—gave a broad array of answers: capital, effective management, positive cash flow, etc. The correct answer was customers. The financial success of any organization is dependent on a good and sustained customer base. Many businesses have painfully learned this when they invested heavily in a great product idea and found that no one wanted it enough to pay for it.

Meeting customer needs is critical to your success as a leader. Time spent learning about your clients and, where possible, hearing directly from them about opportunities and challenges will be extremely helpful in developing ideas for new products, processes, or services. Helping your customers understand the full range of products and services that your company provides may lead to new sales. Through existing relationships, it can be much simpler to convince current clients to buy additional products and services than it is to attract new clients.

Ensuring that your team understands the company's customer base is critical to having a market-driven approach. You can better meet your customers' needs if you understand how they use your products and services in serving their own client base. Learning the opportunities and challenges that their industries are experiencing can be the basis for developing new business lines or preparing for possible changes in sales. Measuring your actions against customer needs will lay the foundation for successful outcomes for your company.

Do your customers see your company's products as value added and are they willing to pay a higher cost for quality? Or do they see your products more as commodities to be purchased from the vendor with the lowest cost? Is your client base made up of a number of different types of clients who come to you for different reasons? Does your company segment its market? If so, does your company have specific strategies for meeting the needs of each segment?

How strong is your company's customer loyalty? Can your company depend on its major clients being there for the long haul, or does it need to consistently replace clients? What are the issues these customers are facing, and how will they affect your company's financial stability? Would you define these issues as risks or as opportunities? If you see them as risks, what could your company do to transform them into opportunities? Is your company's strategic direction market driven and is it based on a realistic understanding of its clients?

Maintaining and expanding your company's customer base is critical for the financial health of your company. Gain access to and study quantitative analyses on your customers. Share these analyses with lower-level management and employees so they will understand who your company's customers are, what their needs are, how they view your company, and why they choose to buy from your company. Is it due to the quality, cost, and/or technological superiority of your products and/or the service your company provides? Does your company measure client satisfaction on a regular basis, in a meaningful and useful manner, and does it monitor the trends affecting your client base? Does senior management keep in close contact with clients and report back in a consistent quantitative manner? How can you translate the available customer information into knowledge that will drive your business area?

How does your company focus on improving its products and services to better meet its client needs? Continuing to provide products and services at the current level will lead a company to failure, so management must constantly work to better meet the needs of its customers to sustain client satisfaction. What are the implications for action for your business area? How can you use this information to be more effective in achieving your goals and contributing to the success of the overall corporation?

Who are your company's competitors, and how do your clients see them in comparison to your company? What are the strengths and weaknesses of each competitor? How effectively does your company compete with each competitor? How is each competitor evolving, and how will all of those changes impact your company's competitiveness? What can you and your function do to help the company compete more effectively?

Do you understand how your competitors' products and services differ from those of your company? How, for example, do your competitors price their products, and what level of customer service do they provide? What is their market niche, and how does it compare to your company's? Study your competitors' promotional materials and products to understand how they position themselves and strategize about how your company can respond. Find publicly available metrics on your competitors' operations and customer satisfaction and compare them with your company's measurements. This will help you identify areas of potential change or improvement.

Does your company collect information on its competitors and distribute this information to the staff to keep everyone aware of the competitive threat? Do you make understanding your competition a high priority for you and your team, whether or not your department has direct customer contact?

When you begin to understand the answers to the questions we have discussed, you will find you can participate more effectively in the active management of the company. You will find you will begin to think and talk differently about the business and will view the role of your business area differently.

Make Business Acumen a High Priority:
In Summary

- Commit to mastering financial skills.
- Gain financial competency.
- Understand the fundamentals of your company's finances.
  - Identify your company's cash requirements and sources.
  - Discover how your company makes and loses money.
  - Understand the financial goals and the financial culture of your company.
  - Know the financial decision makers.
- Know your company's customers and competitors.

Make the Numbers Your Allies

Financial reports are one of the most overlooked sources of critical information about your company, your customers' companies, and your competition. These reports provide insight into the company's goals and performance. When you understand and regularly read these documents, you will have the tools to develop an in-depth understanding of your company or any other company. Most people do not know how to read financial reports and try to hide it. Although women often believe they are less knowledgeable about these reports, it turns out that this is not a function of gender.

The women we interviewed used a wide variety of strategies for acquiring financial skills. They did research on their own—searching the Internet, reading books, and investing in courses. Some took advantage of courses and seminars on financial management. Most developed relationships with experts in their companies who enthusiastically shared their knowledge and wisdom about company finances. A number believed financial management was so important to meeting their professional goals that they returned to school for a master of business administration (MBA) or some other relevant degree. Like Laura, once women find that they understand how to read the stories the numbers told, they begin to really enjoy the business of the business.

Diahann told us, "The reality is, when I was growing up, I hated math. I absolutely hated math. I was always in the accelerated programs, so it was really a pain. When I was in college, I took a math course—I can't remember the specific course, but it was like a calculus for business course—and the light went on. All of a sudden I could see how the advanced math could be useful. I could see an application. So I think in many ways the challenge we have is in providing a link from the numbers to their use as a tool versus their use being the end result."

Diahann advises that one of the best ways of dealing with financial information is to create metrics that work for you. Identify specific elements within your budgets that become triggers if they get to a specific level. Determine the actions you need to take if those levels are reached. For instance, a manager may know that if her sales numbers go up to a certain point, it is a trigger for her to review the expenses associated with them. "Part of it is just having the self-confidence to figure that out," concludes Diahann Lassus.

The ability to understand financial reports is a vital skill for effective business leaders. This knowledge helps you understand your company's financial position and informs the actions you take as a manager. Remember, the numbers tell a story, and the story should drive more informed decisions.

Getting too involved in the details of the numbers can be a distraction that can make you miss the impact of critical trends and relationships. Instead, looking at numbers at a higher level will provide a more useful perspective. Some get caught up in the details and aren't able to move back to a level where they can really see the big picture of what the numbers say. Getting too focused on the details of expenses, for example, can result in your not seeing how expenses and revenue relate. It is important to remember that your job is to understand the stories, not the details.

Conquer Financial Statements

Many successful women began their education on financial reports by reading books in order to have a basic level of understanding before they approached others for assistance. Many books on the subject exist, and a good book can provide a sound foundation of knowledge.

Financial reports strike terror in many managers. As you will see below, however, once you understand the story the reports are telling you about the company's finances and management decisions, you will find that these reports are not as complicated as you may have feared.

Appreciate the Purpose of Each Financial Report
There are four standard reports a company prepares: an income statement, a balance sheet, a cash flow statement, and a statement of retained earnings. These four reports are interrelated and give you the information necessary to follow the money.

- *Income statement.* It tells you whether the company made or lost money during a specific period of time. It shows the company's revenues and expenses, calculating the net profit or net loss. Income statements can also include a calculation of earnings per share. This calculation tells you how much money shareholders would receive for each share of stock they own if the company paid out all of its net income for that period. Income statements report whether a company made a profit.
- *Balance sheet.* It provides detailed information on the assets, liabilities, and shareholders' equity as of a specific date. Assets are shown as current and long-term. Current assets include assets that can change rapidly, such as cash, accounts receivable, and inventory. Long-term assets represent assets that will last for a period of years, such as real estate, equipment, and intellectual

property. Liabilities are shown as current (owed within the year) and long-term (owed after one year). Shareholders' equity is shown in the liabilities section because it represents the money that is owed to the shareholders/owners. Basically, the shareholders' equity represents the book value of the company should all of the assets be sold and the liabilities paid off. The remainder represents the money that would be owed to the shareholders.

- *Cash flow statement.* It reports the cash coming into and going out of the company. As discussed above, the health of a company's cash flow can provide valuable insights into the company's short-term and long-term viability. Cash flow statements can tell you whether the company generated cash.

- *Statement of retained earnings.* It reports what part of net income the company retained rather than distributed to shareholders. These funds are retained to reinvest in the company and provide cash flow. This report is based on information from the income statement. The report shows the changes in shareholders' equity since the last report by adding net income or subtracting net losses from operations and investments and payment of dividends to shareholders.

Use the Standard Financial Ratios

It is important to acquire the ability to apply standard financial ratios resulting from the comparison of numbers from the financial reports. For the uninitiated, ratios may appear to require skills in higher mathematics, and many managers do not even attempt to understand them. In fact, these ratios are relatively simple guidelines to measure a company's health—or lack thereof. Once you understand what ratios signify a healthy organization and what ratios indicate areas that should be explored further, ratios will begin to seem very simple and useful.

A healthy cash-to-debt ratio, for example, in some industries is 1.5 or more. So, if you divide the sum of cash plus short-term investments by the sum of short- and long-term debt and the resulting ratio is lower than 1.5, the company may be vulnerable. It may be carrying too much debt and cannot afford the cost of carrying it. On the other hand, if you find that the ratio is much greater than 1.5, the company may be carrying too little debt, thus missing opportunities for growth or underfunding its growth. Compare your company's ratios with the average ratios for your industry and with the ratios for your company's competitors. This will give you insight into the health of the company and of your competitors. If your competitors are doing better than your company, you may want to do some work to figure out what they are doing and what you can learn from them.

These ratios are guidelines only. A ratio that differs from the standard guideline should not immediately be assumed to indicate problems. Instead, these ratios tell you a story that you need to investigate. A dramatically different ratio may merely be the result of a different strategic approach by management. For instance, a company that keeps a great deal of cash on hand because it believes this gives it a competitive advantage often shows a ratio much higher than 1.5. Instead of indicating a problem, this higher ratio demonstrates that the company is managing its finances consistent with its strategic plan.

This is only one example of a ratio that helps you see the story in the numbers. There are other ratios that are critical to follow based on your industry. Identify the important ratios for your industry and use them to add to the story.

Don't Skip the Interesting Details

In audited financial reports, there are sections that managers should read and understand. Use your internal financial advisors to help you understand what you can learn from these disclosures and how you should use the information in your job.

Always read the footnotes. Auditors are required to provide information important to understanding the numbers presented in these statements. These footnotes provide additional insights into the financial health of the organization. In the footnotes, you will find descriptions of accounting policies and practices that most often impact the portrayal of the company's financial position. These footnotes will also include information on income taxes, obligations to pension and other retirement plans, and stock options. In general, the fewer footnotes, the cleaner the report is.

Learn about management's take on the company's financial position by reading the section entitled "Management's Discussion and Analysis of Financial Condition and Results of Operations" (MD&A). In this section, management has the opportunity to provide investors their analysis of the company's financial performance and their view of the company's financial condition. The purpose of this section is for management to provide investors with the information they perceive is necessary for them to understand the financial condition of the company. It also provides information on trends, events, or uncertainties known to management that could affect the company's future financial status.

Make Sure You Have the Metrics You Need to Do Your Job
Ask your finance department to develop the reports you need to monitor the key aspects of your projects. Management theory says you get more of what you measure, so be sure to measure positive outcomes as well as trouble spots.

You don't need to know exactly how the report should be designed. Instead, explain what you are trying to monitor and the key numbers needed for evaluation, and ask the accounting department to develop the report. Work with the designer until you have the numbers you need in a format that tells you the story you need to know. It is important to request additional measurements such as comparisons with last year's and/or last quarter's numbers to test trends.

Keeping your eye on the money is an important part of your job when you move into management. "What financials help you do is focus," says Maria Coyne. "Having the right metrics and measurements provides a road map to measure progress against your goals, set milestones, and make adjustments along the way. They keep you grounded in what you are trying to accomplish."

Always Build the Business Case

In advocating for yourself or your ideas, from a salary increase to a new product line, always develop a business case showing the financial advantage to the company and/or the customer. Businesses exist to return income from investments; be sure you show how the investments you are asking the company to make will improve the company's bottom line.

Make sure your supporting analyses focus on the benefits to the company and, if appropriate, the customer. For instance, you might include how the outcomes of the reorganization of the department you are proposing is projected to result in a 38 percent decrease in staff costs and a reduction in errors of 24 percent.

Monica Luechtefeld says, "One of the greatest challenges is to achieve the balance between investment and return on investment. You have to be able to drive ideas and initiatives that can deliver sales while being respectful of the investment and delivering results to the overall bottom line of the organization." Understanding the financial performance of your company will give you the foundation to effectively respond to this challenge.

Make the Numbers Your Allies: In Summary

- Conquer financial statements.
  - Appreciate the purpose of each financial report.
  - Use the standard financial ratios.
  - Don't skip the interesting details.
  - Make sure you have the metrics you need to do your job.
- Always build the business case.

Your Company Is Not an Island

Become educated about business in general. Macroeconomics affects the day-to-day operations of every business. Stay current on business issues and events and how they affect the business world in general and your company in particular. Build a solid understanding of economics and global economic trends. Understand public policy and regulations that affect your business and your customers and what your company's positions are on these issues.

When Marilyn Johnson decided she needed to become better informed about business issues and trends affecting the economy so she would "come off more businesslike," she chose to begin her education one step at a time. She started small with the goal of each day reading the front page of the *Wall Street Journal* and one full business article. "Starting out with an easy goal got me in the habit of being informed." From there, she identified columnists to read regularly and began to follow trends in her industry, her territory, and her accounts. Today, she reads voraciously in the fields of business, economic trends, technology, and leadership.

Create Exceptional Teams

As corporations seek to become more nimble in response to the changing global economy, the team building skills that you, as a woman, bring to the organization are becoming more valued. There has never been a more opportune time than today to recognize, value, and own your woman's leadership strengths.

Today, effective team building is on chief executive officers' lists of the top 10 skills they are looking for in up-and-coming executives. From senior management on down, leaders are recognizing that the best results come from diverse, multidisciplinary teams. These may be established functional teams or ad hoc teams brought together for a specific purpose and then disbanded. Senior executives value leaders who know how to work effectively as members of teams, who can build high-performing teams, and who understand what makes teams work and how to get the best out of the teams. These are the very skill areas in which women excel.

Today, the requirement for team building skills goes beyond building a team of people who report to you. Increasingly, senior executives say one of the most valuable skills is the ability to mobilize people who do not report to you in pursuit of a common goal.[1]

Whether you are building an ongoing operational team or an ad hoc team, the principles are the same. At every level, your team is the foundation of your success. The only way to accomplish something really big is to mobilize a large number of people who want to be part of the project. While you may have the idea and the vision, it takes a team of people with a diverse range of expertise and capabilities who share your passion, are committed to a common purpose, and are focused on shared goals to turn your vision into reality. Your job is to bring together the right people, put them in the right positions, provide them with the necessary resources, inspire them, coach them, support them, create structure, and remove the obstacles. You have to reward the high performers and hold accountable those who have not performed at their highest potential.

Be the Orchestra Conductor, Not the Tuba Player

Your role is to be the one who brings the team together to create a symphony, not the one who tries to play every instrument very well. It's the principle of "Learn and Let Go" from Success Strategy Three, "Be the Architect of Your Career." You have to make the transition from being the top individual performer to being the leader who orchestrates the performance of a group of people to create a result that is greater than that of any individual acting alone.

This means you have to be willing to give up the satisfaction of doing the one or two things that you do superbly. It means trusting others to do those things that you do so well. One of women's strengths is their commitment to providing quality products and services. Conversely, one of the things that can hold them back is believing that the best way to ensure this level of quality is to stay personally involved in every aspect of the day-to-day operations. When you stay involved to that level, you end up doing so many things that you are not doing any of them well, and no one is leading the integration of all the parts. The result is that *you* become the greatest barrier to the growth and success of your project or function.

The most fulfilling part of leadership comes when you realize that you will have your greatest impact by establishing a culture that promotes quality and engages every team member in delivering at the highest levels of performance. Once you have accomplished this, you need to let go. Release the day-to-day operations to the team, and empower members of the team to do their jobs and contribute to the success of the organization. Sharon Allen, former Chairman of the Board at Deloitte, LLP, says that when you do this, you are not only helping yourself, you are also giving others the opportunity to gain experience.[2]

This frees you up to do what only you as the leader can do:

- Focus on strategy and direction.
- Engage with customers.
- Ensure that your organization is contributing to the goals of the business at the highest levels.
- Make the linkages between your organization and senior management.

We consistently hear from women at the highest levels that, when you are successful in making this transition, you "fall in love with running the business rather than doing the work of the business, and it is exhilarating."

Create a Culture of Success

When it comes to team building, women have a terrific advantage. Women's leadership styles are collaborative, inclusive, and consultative. They gain commitment by enrolling their team members in achieving a common vision, actively soliciting and listening to employees' ideas, and creating a culture focused on ethical behavior, quality, and concern for the individual. Women leaders recognize that people want to be intellectually stimulated and energized by their environment, to know they are making a valuable contribution, and to be recognized for their performance.

The leader's job is to get everyone enrolled in her vision so that it becomes a shared driving force. Every team member has to be committed to the overall organizational goals rather than to departmental or individual group goals. Choose team members who bring purpose, passion, and commitment to the team's endeavors. Team members who can easily grasp and take ownership of the team's purpose, desired measureable outcomes, urgency, and relevance to the company's strategic goals will contribute at a higher level.

You have to communicate the vision and shared goals time and time again, in multiple ways. Use every communications channel available—meetings, written communications, and voice and video messages. Open up channels of communication using social media techniques to interact with groups within your organization, with individuals, and with the entire team.

Command has given way to collaboration in every modern organization. Judy Robinson says outsiders have the perception that since there is a clear chain of command in the Army, you can just give orders and people will obey you. While you may get action by giving orders, you are getting obedience, not a sense of achieving goals that make a difference. "If that's how you try to lead, you don't get anybody anywhere," says Judy Robinson. "You need to explain to your team why the goal is important. You have to make it a team effort and value what everyone does."

Shared values are a high priority for a team working under time and resource constraints on important issues. Make sure your team members share the values inherent in the project's purpose. As the leader, it is your job to tie together the purpose, values, and importance to the company and the client. Shared values add to the team's cohesion.

Instilling passion to achieve the organization's mission in your team members generates energy and commitment. "Having shared vision and goals really helps create a culture of success," says Maria Coyne. "Part of a culture of success is that you all want to achieve the mission, and working together, you have fun in the process. It doesn't imply that you are just working insane hours—although that happens sometimes—but that you are balanced and having fun and focusing on the right things. Success creates success."

Inspire and Demand Results

As the leader, you provide both inspiration and structure. The Committee of 200 women characterized their leadership styles as energetic, inspiring, and results-oriented. "I have a preference for creating teams that want to grow together and have fun building value for all of our constituents," comments one woman.

One of the most important ways to engage people in their work is to make the work meaningful to them. Take the time to ensure that your team members understand the importance of the work they are doing, how it will be used, and how it will contribute to the success of the company and the client. Teams that believe their work will make a difference are more enthusiastic about their work and work harder to achieve the goal.

Set high standards and ambitious goals, and expect results. Establish a structure of performance evaluations and program reviews as a means of both communicating expectations and recognizing accomplishments. Demand the best from your team, and when people are successful, recognize and reward them.

"While building the business, I focused on creating a winning culture and a passion for success in the people who worked with me. It was important we were all on the same page, and all prepared and ever ready as a team to accomplish our shared objective," says Beverly Holmes. "The first year's success generated enthusiasm for the next year's success. Everyone took pleasure in and enjoyed the energy that being part of a winning team provided. I made every effort to ensure that those who contributed the most to the team's success were recognized and compensated for their contributions. Making sure they knew they were appreciated was a necessary and rewarding business strategy."

Recognize and reward success. When your team has done a good job, let them know. Take the time to celebrate the team's progress and success and to recognize individual performance. In addition to performance evaluations and salary increases when appropriate, take advantage of the company's options for recognition. People love unexpected recognition, even if it is small. A gift certificate to a restaurant or tickets to a ball game or a theater performance let employees know you recognize and appreciate their contributions.

Anne Stevens, Chairman, CEO, and Principal at SA IT Services, characterizes her leadership style as "push, push, hug." She says that you have to set goals that stretch people and be explicit about your expectations. But "you can't push without a hug," says Anne. There has to be a balance. If you do either one without the other, you will be ineffective. "It's setting objectives, and then at the end of the day, recognizing the humanity in all of us."[3]

Show Individuals They Are Valued

In addition to believing that the organizational vision is worth pursuing, employees must perceive that in achieving the organization's goals, they also will be successful in achieving their own personal and professional goals. Take the time to understand what success means to your team members and how you can help them achieve it. Professionally, they may want to gain experience, develop new competencies, and advance in the business. Personally, they may want to have a strong family life and have the resources to fulfill a lifelong dream of organizing a group bicycle tour across Europe. Sometimes learning about employees' personal passions and experience may open up new ways they can contribute to the organization. The same organizational skills that the employee needs to organize a tour may be skills she can apply to a business project. Her knowledge of the countries to be included in her dream tour may be valuable when doing business internationally. Find ways to offer employees experiences and opportunities that contribute to their achieving their professional and personal goals as well as to the organization's success.

The most successful leaders help people recognize their individual strengths. They give them opportunities to use those strengths and build new ones. Employees want to feel they are making progress doing work that is meaningful both to them and to the organization. Reinforce employees' confidence in their skills by putting them in situations where they can perform successfully and then recognizing that performance. Create opportunities for employees to experience success. People who feel successful in their jobs are more creative, productive, and committed, and they make a greater contribution to the overall organization.

One of Laura's managers was sharing her frustrations with Laura about a complex data analysis her team just could not work out. Laura told the employee that while it was difficult, she had total confidence that the team could work it out. An hour later, Laura's phone rang. The elated manager reported that the team had made the analysis work. When Laura told the manager she had known they would succeed, the manager said, "You always believe in us more than we believe in ourselves. Your belief in us is why we succeeded and why I love working here."

One of your most powerful opportunities to engage employees and build a stronger organization comes from knowing how to ask questions and how to listen to the answers. Learn from your employees. Ask for their opinions and how they would do things differently. When you engage each person openly and honestly, you demonstrate that you value the person as well as learn about possibilities and potential you would not have imagined on your own. Solicit employees' ideas and input, discuss their suggestions, and consider their recommendations. The important thing is not whether you adopt an employee's recommendation, but whether the employee feels you have listened seriously, considered the comments, and explained your actions. Be certain to let the employee know when you adopt her or his suggestion or include it in a report or action plan that goes to upper management. This is part of the employee's reward.

People want to be part of a team where people care about each other as individuals as well as coworkers, and the leader sets the tone. Warren Bennis, in his book *On Becoming a Leader*, writes that great leaders lead with empathy—they care for each of their team members as a whole person rather than as a cog in the work process. One of women's strengths is that they bring a holistic perspective to their relationships with others, whether in the work environment, the community, or the family. Laura says you have to realize people do not check their personal lives outside the door when they come to work.

"All leaders need to think about their employees as a family," says Judy Robinson. "It should not be you as the leader looking down on them; it is looking out for them. It means I am concerned about them on all levels."

Be a Positive Role Model to Create Positive Energy

Leaders inspire by example. Be the role model for the behavior you want from your managers and your employees. The way you treat people and the values reflected in your decisions, whether large or small, set the tone for the entire organization. Your emotions are contagious. "Positive energizers create and support vitality in others,"[4] says Kim Cameron, the Associate Dean for Executive Education at the University of Michigan.

Research shows what most women know intuitively—focusing on the positive rather than the negative generates success. One of the most important factors in high-performing groups is a preference for positive and supportive communications. In the Committee of 200 survey, these very successful women business leaders used words and phrases such as "energetic," "positive," "inspirational," and "telling the truth fearlessly" to describe their leadership styles.

It is so easy to be distracted by the challenges and the problems, and successful leaders do not ignore these. However, they do not dwell on them. Negatives carry more weight and last longer in people's memories than positives, adversely affecting attitudes, behavior, and performance. One negative statement in the midst of multiple compliments or one loss in the midst of many successes has a disproportionately greater influence on the organization's culture and individual performance than the successes.[5] In fact, negative interactions had five times as much impact on employees as the positive interactions.[6] Employees who are given negative feedback tend to focus on what went wrong rather than what went right. They begin to lose confidence in themselves and the team, and, worst of all, begin to lose their passion for achieving the organization's goals.

The most successful leaders:

- Create a positive climate.
- Identify and emphasize the organization's strengths and potential.
- Recognize and share with others the value of the group's work.

Laura says she always took the time to focus on the successes to analyze what went right and to reinforce the actions that led to success. When her company won government contracts, she would go to the contracting officer, ask for a debriefing to understand what worked, and then share it with her team. Other companies asked for debriefings only when they lost. Laura found contract officers were more forthcoming when she asked, "How could we have done better?"

Building a culture where employees and managers trust one another is critical. In the Committee of 200 survey, 85 percent agreed that "trust is the emotional capital of business." Trust takes time to build. It is based on shared ethics and values, and must be purposefully cultivated and continuously nurtured through actions and decisions. Trust is fragile and can be destroyed instantaneously with one act. To nurture trust, you must act consistently with your stated values in everything you do and in all your communications.

This is one of those areas where actions speak louder than words. "Your credibility in your organization is built on your past performance," says Camye Mackey. "People know your past accomplishments; they know you have made tough decisions in the past, and this helps you have credibility moving forward." Your reputation precedes you and is continually being built.

Create a Fearless Team
Where Members Are Not Afraid to Fail

Create a culture where informed risk taking is rewarded and failures are accepted as necessary to achieve change. In today's volatile and unpredictable business environment, you have to constantly be examining new ideas and trying new approaches just to stay current and sustain peak performance. Often you are shaking up old, tried-and-true ways of operating. You have to be ready to lead a team that will pursue change, even when everything seems to be running smoothly. Putting forth big, new ideas and moving from the status quo takes courage. Make sure the teams you lead are comfortable with the risk taking necessary for innovation and creativity.

If you want people to take risks, you have to be supportive if the risk does not pay off. Separate the failure from the individual. When employees try new things, they invest high levels of energy, imagination, and time. Sometimes they become so caught up in a new project that they are unwilling to let go of it, even when it is clear that the project is not viable.

You have to monitor progress on new projects, and if it becomes clear that the project is not going to succeed or will require resources beyond your ability to commit them, you have to make the tough decision to stop the project. Often in today's rapidly changing business world, you do not have the luxury of months of pilot testing and debugging. Accept that you may have to implement a new approach before all the "bugs" have been resolved. Have a fallback plan ready just in case. Help employees understand and accept the possibility of failure, as well as the joy of experimenting and learning.

Employees often are disappointed when a project they have worked hard on does not fulfill its promise. In this case, it is particularly important to help the employees who were working on the project deal with their disappointment and recognize that the failure is not personal.

Let them know you recognize it was not they as individuals who failed, it was the project. Reinforce that they remain valued team contributors. Recognize and celebrate the individuals for being willing to take the risk. When risk taking is rewarded, people become better at recognizing what risks will pay off. They have a sense of purpose and determination, and are ready to deal with the possibilities.

Coach team members to constantly analyze their expertise and skills to make sure they are updating and refining their competencies. These are the people who will grow with the organization and keep it vibrant. Work with them to develop an ongoing strategy for updating their skills and expertise.

Seek out team members who are curious and committed to life-long learning. These people are invaluable to the team's productivity and willingness to take risks. Curiosity leads to innovation. It brings excitement to projects and makes work more fun.

Successful risk takers have critical thinking skills. Team members with these skills are more likely to examine assumptions, seek out and evaluate evidence, clarify goals, and test conclusions. Critical thinking skills increase the likelihood the team will produce high-quality outcomes that contribute to the company's strategic goals.

Choose team members with common sense. This is one of the most difficult skills to find, yet the people with common sense bring an important perspective to the team. These are the team members who help the team avoid overly complicated and impractical approaches. They understand the implications of actions, and they help the group develop simple, workable strategies. These are the team members whom you will pay attention to when they ask, "Is there a reason why we are doing . . . ?"

Create a Culture of Success: In Summary

- Inspire and demand results.
- Show individuals they are valued.
- Be a positive role model to create positive energy.
- Create a fearless team where members are not afraid to fail.

Hire the Best

The people you choose for your team are the lifeblood of your business. Surround yourself with really smart people, smarter than you. It takes a great deal of self-confidence to hire people who are better than you in their area of expertise. It takes even more self-confidence to hire someone better than you to do the jobs where you excel and that you enjoy doing. However, once you have brought these people into the organization, you will find you appreciate the benefits of having people who bring superior skills. Bring in people who complement your skills and knowledge, and fill in gaps in your knowledge or experience.

Hire Slowly

You are going to have to work with your team members every day, invest in coaching and training them, and go to the mat for them if necessary. Select people you are excited to see every day, who stimulate you, and whom you enjoy having around you. Make certain they fit in with the team's culture, buy into the vision, and will contribute to achieving the organizational goals.

Spend a lot of time hiring. While subject matter knowledge and professional information are important, you want people who know how to make things happen and when confronted with barriers, figure out a way around them. Seek people who are intellectually curious and have good judgment when confronted with alternatives. Look for people who have the ability to seek out, evaluate, and synthesize information. You want someone who will take work off your desk.

Look for people who know how to be team players and contribute to the success of the entire organization. It is easy to be carried away by top talent, but if the person does not know how to work effectively with others, the value of the talent ends up being lost to the team.

Hire Strategically

Fill openings strategically. An opening is an opportunity to build for the future. Think about where your organization is going and how it is changing. What skills and experience will you need as the organization grows, the mission evolves, and the market changes? Ask yourself what you think the person you hire will be doing in three years. Hire so you will be prepared to move ahead nimbly when new opportunities present themselves.

When you hire, you should consider succession planning for key positions in the organization. At the time that high-potential people are ready to move on or an opportunity opens up, you have the responsibility to have their successors and replacements in the pipeline. "Be prepared for the moment when you want to promote someone. It is difficult if there is not a successor clearly identified to step into their place," says Monica Luechtefeld. "I set a high priority on working with my teams to identify and develop successors so I can continue to move high performers up in the organization."

Provide Coaching and Mentoring

Having the right people in the right positions is only part of the job. "As a leader, you have the responsibility to clearly articulate a vision, ensure that people know the role they are going to play and what is expected of them, and then give them good coaching and mentoring to help them develop," says Monica Luechtefeld.

Successful leaders ensure that people know the role they play in the organization and what is expected of them. While the top women business leaders view themselves as inspiring and energizing leaders, they are clear that they also are demanding and expect results. "It helps people when we set the parameters and hold them accountable for achieving their responsibilities," says Camye Mackey.

The best leaders believe it is their responsibility to be both a coach and a mentor to their people. Your role, they say, is to help your employees develop the ability to think through problems creatively, come up with new ideas, take ownership of implementation, and make independent decisions. The result is you are empowering them to make decisions on their own, and they can act and operate independently. Camye Mackey says, "It comes down to knowing the people you work with, their style, and what motivates them so you can lead them to exceptional performance. It is critical to provide clear expectations, coaching and feedback, and rewards and recognition. You need to know how to reward and encourage great performance, turn around mediocre performance, and exit continued poor performance."

You should provide assignments to stretch people beyond their comfort zone and master new skills. By expressing your confidence in them, you help them gain self-confidence, believe in themselves, and believe in their abilities.

At the same time, provide a safety net. Usha Pillai says one of the best compliments she ever received was from a new manager who reported to her. "Usha, I don't know how you do this. You let me go to the edge, but you make sure I don't fall off the cliff." Prior to a cross-divisional meeting, he had come to Usha with his strategy, and they had debated it. Instead of telling him she disagreed with his approach, she asked if he had considered an alternative approach that she then described. At the meeting, he realized that, given the current business situation, her recommended strategy was the correct one. Thus he gained credibility with the team and realized the value of rethinking an approach.

Usha continues, "My job was to position him to be successful at the meeting and be seen as the primary contact. I didn't want the team to come back to me for the final decision." Her trust in him and his willingness to take the information she had given him and make the call gave him the confidence to make decisions and take ownership of the project. The results benefited the individual, the team, and ultimately the company by developing future leaders.

Fire Fast

Every successful businesswoman's mantra is, "Hire slowly; fire fast." Take time to ponder the hiring decision, but make the decision on the people who are not performing or do not fit in with the organizational culture quickly and move them out. You want to believe you can turn this person around. "In the early days, I always had the hope that I could energize and enroll everyone in new strategies or initiatives, but I finally realized that is not always possible, and sometimes the person just needs to change organizations," says Monica Luechtefeld.

When you address these situations, you are benefiting the employee as well. Employees who cannot be successful in their current position need to move to an organization where they can be successful. Free them up to find a job where success is within their reach.

Beverly Holmes agrees. There were people hired into the business who could not embrace her hard-driving, unwavering, focused approach on exceeding annual goals. "One of my hard-learned leadership lessons was that you have to let those people go and quickly, even if they were sent to you by a dear colleague or your best friend. Once negativity starts infiltrating the culture, you start to see and hear dissention, which is a dividing tool that can and will undermine your efforts to succeed and lead to changing the focus from the work and business needs to the perceived problem. Removing the distraction early also demonstrates a lack of tolerance for unhealthy attitudes which threaten the continued success of your operation."

Leaders like to focus on developing and grooming the superstars. But research finds that all the good that is achieved by having a high-performing superstar can be canceled out by even one "bad apple." That one "bad apple" reduces organizational performance by 30 to 40 percent.[7] If the superstar is the disruptive one, move her or him out. The disruptive behavior outweighs the value of the individual's performance. In fact, overall productivity will increase when the disruptive individual is removed from the team, even if no one employee can perform at the same level as the superstar.

Everyone knows who is performing and who is not. Your credibility as the leader increases when you take action. As for the employee, often she or he realizes this is not the right position, but is afraid to take the first step to move on. Position the situation as a mismatch between the needs of the organization and the individual's strengths. Present moving on as an opportunity to explore new opportunities more suited to the individual's strengths.

Hire the Best: In Summary

- Hire slowly.
- Hire strategically.
- Provide coaching and mentoring.
- Fire fast.

Be a Team Player Yourself

In addition to leading your own team, you are always part of other teams. You are part of your manager's team. You may sit on permanent committees such as a new business review committee. There are always the ad hoc committees to address an emerging challenge, develop new initiatives, or prepare the company's response to an unexpected business situation. The more senior you become, the more likely you are to be a member of these ad hoc committees.

Being a team player has a negative connotation in some people's minds. If being a team player is interpreted to mean that you will not raise questions about the team leader's ideas or state your concerns about company practices and policies, that you will go along to get along, then being a team player is indeed negative. Today, being a team player is a way to be a force for positive change in the company. You cannot afford to be viewed as an extreme maverick or a loner.

You not only have to know how to build and lead teams, but also have to know how to be an effective, active contributor as a team member. Be ready to contribute your best ideas and insights to the team. Encourage and support the exchange of ideas and perspectives of fellow team members. Recognize there is value in using your position as a respected team player to be part of the leadership that is strengthening and leading the company. As companies increasingly turn to ad hoc teams to make decisions and manage change, having team skills positions you to be part of the recognized pool of top talent.

Nurture Your Greatest Asset—You

Invest in yourself so you can be the best that you can be. Successful women love both their work and their families. They want to be active in the community, and they know they need to take care of themselves physically, spiritually, and intellectually. But, they realize they cannot be everything to everybody at the same time, and that's okay. They realize they do not have to do everything themselves. The key to making your life doable and fun is establishing priorities and living by them.

Integrate Your Life; Balance Is a Myth

Loving what you do is important. Your work provides satisfaction and purpose, challenges to energize you, and accomplishments to celebrate in the professional part of your life. "But you also need some distance and detachment so you are not so caught up in your work you cannot see the things around you," says leadership expert Nannerl Keohane, who was the first woman president of Duke University. If you make work your entire life, you are very likely to end up hollowed out because you do not have any other sources of joy in your life. "You need for your own success, to be a person who has a better-rounded sense of life toward work and sets examples for those around you," says Dr. Keohane.[1]

Notice that she uses the term *better-rounded*, not balanced. Balance is a myth that has been foisted off on women. The concept of a perfectly balanced life, with family, work, community, and personal life in equilibrium, is unrealistic and not as fulfilling as the myth suggests. What we have learned is that successful businesswomen focus on integrating their personal and professional lives by setting priorities based on their values.

Set Priorities

Your values and goals are the foundation for integrating your personal and business lives. Based on your values, you have to decide what aspects of your life take precedence at different times—children, husband or partner, business, community responsibilities, or personal life. These are not priorities you set on the fly without thought and consideration. You need to consider what is important and when it is important. Be very specific. Discuss priorities with your family and trusted business advisors. Don't assume you know what is important to your family or your business.

Ask your family members what is most important to them. Think about your personal life. Think about the importance of time with friends or to invest in your well-being. It is often being there for the small things in life that is most important. You may be surprised at what is important to the significant people in your life. Sharon was. When she talked to her husband, she learned it wasn't her travel or late nights at the office. Instead, it was his classic car hobby events. The most important thing for him was for her to attend the car shows with him. After that discussion, the annual car show schedule was on Sharon's work calendar, and everyone knew those dates were inviolate.

Laura faced the challenge of caring for a child who was very ill and running a company at the same time. She needed to continue to work, yet be available to her son on a moment's notice. She and her managers discussed what aspects of her job it was critical that she continue to handle and what could be transferred to them. As a result, Laura was able to fulfill both professional and family responsibilities.

Laura's clients also were aware of the challenges she was facing, and it was an experimental medicine being developed by one of her clients that cured her son. She says the experience also taught her how work complements and supports your personal life when you are faced with personal challenges. "Prior to this experience, I would have told an employee to take time off and focus on her child," says Laura. "Now I understand having work to distract me made me feel I could be effective when I felt so impotent with my son's situation. Work helped me keep my emotional stability."

The women we have interviewed say the key to the best solution is in your approach. In the past, women felt they had to choose between their career and their family. Some chose to drive ahead in their profession and either deferred or chose not to have a family. Others dropped out of the workforce for a time and then returned to build a rewarding career. As we discussed in Success Strategy Two, "Own Your Destiny," thanks to the changes in the way we work, more options are available to women today that make integrating family and work life easier. These options also help women avoid large breaks in their careers.

One option that offers the most promise is flexible work arrangements. When flexible work arrangements were first introduced, the common perception was that women who took advantage of them were signaling a lack of commitment to their career and advancement. But successful women have helped to reposition their desire for flexibility as just the opposite—as a signal that they are committed to their career and advancement and therefore want to stay active in the workforce and the company. They are taking the initiative to create and propose solutions specifically tailored to their current position that will allow them to fulfill work commitments and personal priorities.

Think of this as a unified integration of work and family, not a juggling act. Adopt the approach that there is a solution that serves the needs of both family and business. It is your responsibility to take the lead in identifying that solution. You need to know what you want, be creative in how you approach the challenges, and, most of all, ask for the flexibility you need and be open to negotiation.

Kate Nealon recalls that she and her husband discussed what was important to them at the beginning of their marriage. She says, "It was very important to both of us to have children. But my husband also thought if a woman stays home with her children full time and never goes back to work, that creates a great big divide in the marriage. He really felt that you wouldn't be able to share as many things." To make two high-powered careers work required that they both commit to the same priorities around raising the children and managing family, and both be committed to being available to step in when the other could not.

Understanding the values of your business culture and your family means knowing when it is and is not okay to have someone cover for you. When you build your team, make certain you have leaders who can represent your function at key meetings and work on ensuring that they have the credibility to attend meetings on your behalf. Discuss priorities with your manager and let her or him know how you will handle a situation when you have to arrive late, leave early, or take off for a school event or soccer game.

This is when you realize how critically important it is to consider company values when choosing a place to work. Ask the question, "Will the values of this company support me in fulfilling both my professional and personal goals?" Increasingly, companies are taking into consideration the life goals of both women and men employees in establishing their personnel policies and procedures. As we discussed in Success Strategy Three, "Be the Architect of Your Career," the values of KeyBank are one of the main reasons Maria Coyne continues to work there. When we interviewed Maria, she had just gotten off the telephone with one of her colleagues, a woman who is chief financial officer (CFO) of a major division. The kindergarten graduation ceremony for the CFO's twins was scheduled the same time as she and Maria were expected to be at the management committee presenting their strategy, and the CFO was struggling with the decision about what to do. Maria says she never hesitated before responding, "You know what you have to do. Why are you even questioning this decision? Everyone in that room will know that your place is to be at that graduation."

Ask for What You Want

When confronted with an attractive business opportunity that on the surface seems incompatible with your personal commitments, do not just sigh and turn it down. Figure out what would allow you to do both and develop a proposal showing the benefit to the company. Almost everything is negotiable if you simply ask.

Kate Nealon was offered the position as Group Head of Legal and Compliance at Standard Chartered Plc., a large global multinational banking institution. The position had always been based in London. However, she had only recently found a school where her dyslexic son was progressing well, and she wanted to remain in New York. So, she proposed that she do the job from New York, offering to spend one week a month in London and other global capitals. Management agreed, albeit reluctantly, since they had never had a position of this stature located outside London. It turned out being located in New York worked well because Kate's travel often was to bank locations other than London, such as Hong Kong, Singapore, India, and Africa. For two and a half years, she traveled one week a month. Subsequently Kate did transfer to London; however, it was on her schedule.

You have to take the initiative to address conflicts that arise between your personal and professional lives. It is surprising how often workarounds can be made. Kate Nealon's two children got married within weeks of each other. She says, "You have to get your mind around it. No one is going to tell you to miss your kid's important events. I had a board I just joined move the board meeting because it conflicted with my both my kids' weddings. They probably were wondering 'just how many kids does she have?'"

Integrate Personal and Professional Goals to Achieve Success

Integrating personal and professional goals often drives decisions about career moves. Many of the women we interviewed had adjusted their careers to accommodate personal and family goals and priorities. In every case, what seemed like a detour set them on a different path that led to unforeseen opportunities and highly successful careers.

Monica Luechtefeld left a position she loved as Director of Admissions at Mount St. Mary's College when she decided to have a family because the college position required working evenings and weekends. She joined a small office supplies company because the job there would not require the long hours. This move ultimately resulted in her becoming a leader in the transformation of the office supplies industry and to her current position as Executive Vice President at Office Depot.

When Camye Mackey was pregnant with her second child, a comment from her three-year-old daughter stopped her in her tracks. Her daughter asked, "Mommy, we don't have a whole lot of time to spend together making cupcakes now, so what's going to happen when the baby comes?" Camye says she was torn between a career she loved and wanted to continue and the desire to spend more time at home. "I brainstormed with my husband about how I could have the best of both worlds." Together they realized that she could build on her corporate experience and keep up her presence in the industry by launching her own human resources consulting firm. "I had a ball working with start-up and midsized companies, providing training and assisting them, but still being able to spend more time with my little ones and kind of regroup and refocus." When the children—now numbering three—were older, she returned to corporate America because she liked being in the corporate environment and working and interacting with colleagues. However, the time on her own gave her a different perspective and new priorities. Camye says, "I came back with a new frame of mind and a new priority list. Instead of working harder, I started working smarter because I knew it was important to have that focus for family as well as work."

Laura says having a child dramatically increased the quality of her life because it made her eliminate the things in her life that were not really important or enjoyable. "I loved being with my son so much, I eliminated a lot of commitments I had not realized were not important to me," remembers Laura. "So in all aspects, my life got better."

As we were finishing up this chapter, Laura's youngest son, now a successful adult, said, "Don't forget to add that my Mom won the Mother of the Year award while she was running a business."

Kim Roberts had a well-established career as a journalist, reporter, and producer, primarily covering foreign affairs, when she married a military officer. She knew very little about military life, including the fact that relocation orders often change several times before you actually move, so any career planning for her would be difficult. "I learned that you can't plan ahead because they change it on you, so it is really hard to be a professional and be married to somebody in the military unless you just don't accompany them," says Kim. "But I had decided I was married and why did I get married if I wasn't going with him."

Rather than give up on her professional aspirations, Kim took advantage of each change of station to identify opportunities to add to her credentials, diversify her experience, and expand her expertise. In Okinawa, she became the U.S. Army public relations officer, giving her an opportunity to learn both the military and the local community. When her husband was transferred to Miami, she used the time to earn her doctorate in international relations and get experience teaching at the college level. The combination of her journalistic credentials and her knowledge of military and international strategy positioned her for her current job as Director of Government Analysis at Science Applications International Corporation (SAIC) when she and her husband returned to Washington, D.C. Kim says, "My career hasn't been linear in the traditional sense, but it has been linear in a big picture sense."

Women Conquer the Struggles with Integration

Integrating family and professional lives is a perennial challenge. This quote from one of the respondents in the Committee of 200 survey is a poignant summary of what we regularly hear from successful businesswomen: "My greatest challenge was ensuring that

I was the mom I wanted to be and the business leader I wanted to be—at the same time."

While most of the stories women tell are about the challenges that arise when they try to integrate having children and working, married women without children and single women also struggle with integration. Their challenge often is made more difficult because other people think that since they don't have the responsibility for children, they should take on the longer hours, they don't need the workplace flexibility, or they don't experience the conflict between personal and professional priorities. Regardless of your family status, building a well-rounded, integrated life is the path to fulfillment and success, and benefits such as workplace flexibility are important to *all* women.

Women worry that if they allow personal priorities to affect their business life—or business priorities to affect their personal life—they will miss out on something important. Laura says she always felt guilty about her children when she was focusing on her professional life and felt guilty about her business when she was focusing on her personal life. Sheryl Sandberg, COO of Facebook, says guilt is one of the top impediments to women succeeding in the workforce. Her simple statement reflects what so many women feel, "I feel guilty working because of my kids."[2] And, all women feel guilty when they take time for themselves and their personal priorities.

The research on the impact on the children of mothers' working is conflicting. Some studies report that children with working mothers are less well-adjusted and more likely to have problems in school. Other studies find that children of working moms are just as well-adjusted or better adjusted. It is likely that there are benefits and drawbacks whichever path you choose; the key is to take a positive approach.

The guilt is compounded by the fundamental belief that women are responsible for the home, children, and, in many cases, caring for elderly parents. Corporate executives, spouses or partners, and even the women themselves continue to ascribe to this belief. Women compound the challenge by believing they not only are responsible, but must do it all themselves. "I was trying to be the best housekeeper and the best mother, and the best everything," says Judy Robinson. "And let's face it, you cannot work 24 hours a day."

Husbands or partners often resist when women decide to bring in a housekeeper, even when money is not an issue. After a presentation on business growth to a group of highly successful women business leaders, Sharon was sitting with the group's officers, sipping wine and discussing their greatest challenges. The question these women were struggling with was not how to lead their substantial business operations but, "How did you convince your husband to agree to your hiring a housekeeper?" The responses, some said facetiously, ranged from making him do the laundry so he would realize how much of it there was to threatening to leave him with the children and all the accompanying responsibilities. The most important message in the conversation was the affirmation that—whether you are married or single, with or without children—it is okay to let go and hire others to do the things at home that truly do not require your skills or insights.

Accept That You Cannot Do It Alone

Start by accepting that you cannot do it all yourself. You know that about work—it is why you build a team of experts and establish networks. The most successful businesswomen transfer these leadership insights to their personal life. "One of the things I wish I had known earlier was that I didn't have to do everything myself," says Judy Robinson.

For most highly successful women—whether married with or without children, a single parent, or single without children—one of their most liberating moments was the realization it was not only okay but preferable to hire someone to clean the house or help with childcare. "I was a better mother because instead of cleaning the house when I was home, I could spend time with my son," says Judy Robinson, who for many years of her career was a single parent. Judy also hired in-home house care rather than beating herself up over trying to race her son off to school when she had an early meeting. That way, he could get up at the same time and get on his regular school bus. "All of a sudden, life became so much easier when I took some of the burdens off and realized I was still taking care of those personal areas, just in a different way."

If you are married, make sure "your partner is a real partner," says Sheryl Sandberg.[3] Nina McLemore says that one of the keys to success is to marry well. In the "olden days," this meant marrying a man with money and career potential who would support his wife and children in high style. Today, it means marrying someone who supports your aspirations and is willing to be a full partner in managing your joint personal life. In the Committee of 200 survey, over half (56 percent) of the women said they would not be as successful today as they are if not for their spouse or partner.

When asked what the most important factor in her success is, Kate Nealon responds, "Without a scintilla of a doubt, it's my husband." Throughout her career, Kate worked internationally, in positions often requiring substantial international travel. She says her husband has been "hugely involved in the children's lives. The children saw us as a united parental unit, and there was always one parent on call, which as a joke we called the parent of record. We took turns staying home with an ill child." One or the other would try to get home to see the children before they went to bed. In the morning, they divided up the duties of getting everyone up and ready and making breakfast. They insisted on one weekday night as Family Dinner when they all ate together, and they had all weekend meals together as a family. They worked to schedule their travel so that when one was traveling internationally, the other would be closer to home. She likens their scheduling to running a firm. "Even our holidays were long negotiated," says Kate.

Many women have learned that what is most important is establishing rituals and routines your children can count on. Susan Helstab says she had heard that creating rituals is what gives children a sense of grounding and parental involvement, even if the parent is not always there. So, when she began to travel extensively, she established a ritual bedtime telephone call. "Every single night no matter what time zone I was in I called at her bedtime to say goodnight. It meant we got to speak. That was something she counted on throughout her childhood." Susan's daughter had a children's book called *I'll Love You Forever* that has a recurring paragraph with the message, "I'll love you forever." That paragraph became their ritualized sign-off. Her daughter called the paragraph "the words." "After she told me about her day and she was ready to end the conversation, she would say to me, 'Mommy, say the words,' and I would recite the paragraph as our last words. Later, when she went to camp, she told me she couldn't get to sleep without hearing my voice saying the words." Susan says she learned the important thing was not always being present, but committing to a consistent way of connecting that her daughter could count on.

Laura recorded nighttime stories so her children could have a goodnight story from mom even when she was traveling. The children liked the recordings so much, they listened to them even when she was home.

Talking about the challenges of integrating family and professional responsibilities, Kate Nealon says, "It is not something the world imposes on you. You have to want it, and you have to want it a lot. I don't know if you have to want it more than a man does—I've never been a man. You need to be ambitious in a very similar way, and then make it work out."

Most women report that tools such as an integrated calendar are vital to integrating your life. They allow you to plan your life, not just your business. Camye Mackey says her calendar includes not just business meetings and commitments but also doctors' appointments, school meetings, and events with family and friends. For her, being organized at work is critical to being organized at home. "I have to feel I have accomplished something at the end of the day to make it worthwhile not being at home with the children. If I think about what I wish I had known earlier that I know now, it would be to work smarter, not harder, learn to delegate, and learn to organize yourself professionally and personally."

Women believe the skills they develop as the result of integrating their personal and professional lives offer real benefits to both the workplace and their families. They are experienced at managing complex and diverse schedules; they know how to be flexible, nimble, and resilient; and, most of all, they do not sweat the small stuff. They see themselves as role models—showing their daughters and other young women that a woman can be successful both as a professional and as a parent, and showing their sons that women are business leaders as well as family leaders.

Build a Network to Support
Personal and Professional Integration

Personal networks are as important as your professional networks. You need multiple personal networks just as you need multiple professional networks. The most successful businesswomen have developed networks that help integrate their personal and professional life.

Some of these are networks of family and friends:

- The grandparents, who can pick up the children from school or be the fallback people when the children are sick.
- The neighbor, whom you can call on to help when you cannot get home on time (or when you can't remember if you turned off the burner under the kettle).

Others are networks of paid service providers:

- The pet sitter, who can walk the dog or feed the cat.
- The babysitter, who can drive your child to softball or soccer practice.
- The housekeeper, who can make certain the house is clean and the laundry is done.

"On a personal front, you need a support network," says Maria Coyne. "Everybody has to think about harnessing the power of their personal support network. You think about really high-performing women—and you can joke that it takes a village, but it does. When you think about these successful women, there is often a team behind them helping to get things done in different ways, personally as well as professionally. It's also understanding that you can't do it all yourself."

Integrate Your Life; Balance Is a Myth:
In Summary

- Set priorities.
- Ask for what you want.
- Integrate personal and professional goals to achieve success.
- Accept that you cannot do it alone.
- Build networks to support personal and professional integration.

Invest in Yourself: Your Intellectual, Physical, and Spiritual Well-being

Invest both time and money in your intellectual, physical, and spiritual well-being. Finding the time usually is more challenging than finding the money. Women often tell us they are uncomfortable justifying the time away from family or work to participate in a seminar, go to the gym, or meditate quietly. It is easy to give priority to the time demands of daily work and family, and suddenly find the day is over with no time for investing in yourself.

Become a Lifelong Learner

Highly successful businesswomen make lifelong learning a priority. These women are intellectually curious, always wanting to know about trends, emerging technologies, and management theories. They read voraciously on a wide range of topics—business, social issues, social and economic trends, leadership, creativity, biographies, and fiction. They attend seminars and conferences—to keep current about their industry, to celebrate and learn about women's leadership, to keep up-to-date on world economic and social trends, to open their minds to new ways of thinking, and to be inspired. For example, when we interviewed Marilyn Johnson, she had just returned from a conference exploring the concept of reality and dreams.

The most successful women learn from other business leaders and subject matter experts—both women and men. Their discussions range broadly and are not limited to business leadership. Laura would invite other business leaders or subject matter experts to lunch, and the other leaders would be so flattered by her interest in their area of expertise, they would freely share with her the expertise and insights a consultant would charge thousands of dollars to access. They would share with her the important "lessons learned" they had acquired through experience over the years. The discussions ranged from the pain of terminating senior staff to fears they had during economic downturns. These discussions gave Laura insights on how to handle these issues and reassured her that the stress she was feeling when addressing these problems was normal and not a sign of weakness.

This is what allows you to foresee trends, identify new market opportunities leapfrogging the competition, develop new approaches to business operations, enhance personal skills, and develop personal awareness. In interviews with over 70 executives, the trait they identified as most important to achieving business success is "passionate curiosity." Passionate curiosity goes beyond wanting to learn new things; it is being driven to:

- Understand how and why things work and what would work better.
- Understand and learn from others by asking them what they think, what works for them, and how things can be improved.
- Engage with the world around you and always seek to understand and gain new insights.[4]

Many large corporations have world-class education and training programs. Take advantage of these programs. Marilyn Johnson says she has always been a student. "I always signed up for new classes—in everything from IBM's tools-based basic skills courses to those in leadership, strategy, and the executive education offered at some of the top business schools," says Marilyn. "The executive education classes are priceless. They allow you to push back from the day-to-day routine, assess where you are, set goals to go further, and really invest in listening to experts from different disciplines."

You cannot always count on your employer to provide you with the professional development opportunities you need. "You have to take personal responsibility for professional development, whether it is attending a lecture or conference, tuning into something on the Web, or reading," says Maria Coyne. "There is no shortage of books on any topic these days, and it is very important to keep stretching yourself and thinking. It is incumbent on everybody to continue to invest in themselves professionally as well as personally."

Consider going back to school for specialized programs, such as an executive MBA or a certificate in a particular specialty that complements a professional degree. When Nina McLemore left Liz Claiborne, she returned to school to get a second MBA. Judy Robinson has four advanced degrees—master of international management, master of education, master of strategic studies, and a fellowship in military medical history. Advanced education provides the knowledge that keeps you at the leading edge of your profession and the credentials for new career opportunities.

Invest in Wellness

How many times have you heard someone say about you, "I just don't know where she gets all that energy"? In the Committee of 200 survey, 89 percent of the respondents said that "health is a key ingredient of high performance," and 83 percent affirmed that they exercise for 30 minutes or more at least three times a week.

Invest in your physical well-being. To be the leader you aspire to be at all times takes a high level of energy and wellness. Mary Cantando says, "The ROI on a healthy body can't be overestimated." You cannot live the life you lead as a business leader, mother, wife, daughter, and community leader if you are not in good physical condition.

Make your personal well-being a top priority. Commit yourself to regular exercise routines. This can be as simple as taking a walk in the morning or as formal as going to the gym regularly and working with a trainer. Maria Coyne now adds time to go work out to her calendar. She says if she does not schedule it, it will not happen. But it took her many years to feel confident enough to actually put it on her work calendar. "I work enough hours that I don't have to explain to anyone what I am doing with two hours out of a 66-hour workweek. But it took me some time to be okay with that," says Maria. "Maybe it is a woman thing that we think about ourselves last, and that is not good, because if you are not healthy, you cannot take care of all the other people you are trying to take care of both at work and at home."

Marilyn Johnson talks about the importance of pacing yourself and building in time to take care of yourself. "You cannot borrow or lend time. You only have so much time in the day for rejuvenation, so you need to focus on what you eat and getting your sleep," says Marilyn. She tries to set aside time for a monthly facial, and when she travels, to get a massage or, when attending conferences, to go to a yoga or Pilates class. "You definitely need to allow some latitude so you can keep your sanity when unexpected things happen."

Keep up with medical visits. The challenge with medical appointments is they normally are during the business day, when you already have a full schedule. Put the appointments on your calendar and honor them. Treat your doctors' appointments like your most important business appointments.

Invest in Your Spirituality

The most successful women leaders are in touch with themselves and their inner core. By connecting with your inner energy, they say, you create your own reality, a reality that becomes success.

Investing in your spirituality can run the gamut from formal religion to quiet meditation to keeping a personal journal. Hillary Clinton, speaking at an Office Depot conference for women business leaders not long after the Clintons had left the White House, shared what it took to deal with the challenges of her days as First Lady, especially the criticisms and negative comments. She reported she had learned to practice "intentional gratitude." Every morning before she got out of bed, she would think about the previous day and what she had to be grateful for and then think about what she had to be grateful for in the coming day. Whatever you do, take time for reflection, for recentering yourself, and for giving thanks.

Focusing internally and creating an inner peace gives you self-confidence. It helps you focus on your strengths, deal with adversity, and differentiate what is important from the noise-level distractions.

Build Personal Support Networks

Just as you build networks for business and managing family responsibilities, nurture yourself by building networks of friends and colleagues who will support you emotionally, provide personal advice in the difficult times, and celebrate with you in the good times. Some members of this network may overlap with members of your other networks; others will be completely independent of your other connections.

People in your personal support network are the friends you can call when everything is falling down about your ears and you need to vent. They are the friends who bring over the champagne when you win and want to celebrate. Sometimes, it is a friend you have lunch or a glass of wine with once every few months, whether you need to or not.

Many times your personal networks will be groups of like-minded women who come together to learn from each other and support one another. These are groups where you can ask the questions you don't want to admit you have, share your doubts, exchange personal as well as business advice, celebrate both your personal and professional accomplishments, and have a good laugh about the crazy things that happen in everyday life. These may be formal or informal groups. Camye Mackey, for example, has a group of girlfriends she takes a trip with every year, a time just for them to have fun and refresh themselves.

Treat Your Time and Energy as Scarce and Valuable Resources

Treat your time and energy as resources that are as scarce and critical as any item in your business or household budget. This means being strategic about what you will do and will not do and having the courage to say "no."

In business, it means identifying those responsibilities that only you can do or that you, as the leader, must do because of your position. As we discussed in Success Strategy Six, "Build Exceptional Teams," it is tempting to continue to do the things you do very well even if others can take them over. You have to focus on leadership responsibilities—strategy, external relationships, and team leadership. These are where you make a unique difference to the organization. Release all other responsibilities to members of your team, even if they are things you love to do. When you do this, you not only open up your time to be spent where it will have the greatest impact, but motivate others by giving them new responsibilities, demonstrate your confidence in their abilities, and create commitment to the organization.

Learn to say "no" when assignments are added to an already heavy workload. If you always accept additional assignments and perform regardless of the extra hours required, you will be expected to always say "yes." This is the curse of the competent. Competent people make it look easy to do the impossible.

Evaluate whether the assignment will provide you with opportunities you would not otherwise have. Don't assume you have to do it if you want to get ahead. Ask yourself if it is worth the extra time and energy it will take from other work, your family, or your personal commitments.

Discuss the assignment with your manager and ask about the benefits for you. Share your current workload. If you believe this is a valuable opportunity, discuss renegotiating your current workload. If you believe this is not the best use of your time and energy, recommend someone else who could do it and make the case why that person would be better suited for the assignment. If you say "no" at the right times, you actually create a positive impression and engender respect.

Use the same rationale of focusing on what only you can do for your time at home, with your family, or in the community. If a task does not require your personal skills and attention, hire someone else to do it. Save your time and energy to be a special friend, a sister, mother, wife, or daughter, and to take care of yourself. That is where you make a unique difference to your family and for yourself.

One of the greatest challenges to using your time and energy strategically is responding to requests from the community and special groups, especially women's groups. As a woman of achievement, you are viewed as a role model, a representative of all women—as in "We need a woman's perspective." Successful women are sought-after to join boards, participate on business committees, and speak—especially to women's groups. Indeed, the more successful you are, the more others seek your advice and assistance. They present you with awards and feature you in their newsletters. In addition, they often expect you to buy a table, sell tickets, or share your contact list.

These requests come from worthy groups, including community leaders, for-profit and nonprofit organizations, customers, employees, business colleagues, and aspiring women business leaders. The invitations are flattering and often you believe in the cause or the goals of the organization. Thus it is hard to turn down the multiple requests without feeling guilty.

However, time and energy are not infinite. This goes back to the importance of establishing priorities based on your personal and professional values and goals. Choose the opportunities that are most meaningful to you, where you can make the greatest contribution, or that advance your professional goals. You will have a much greater impact if you focus your time and energy on a few strategic opportunities than if you scatter your attention over a broad but unconnected group of organizations and committees. Take into account the demands of both your business and personal life as you establish priorities. There may be a time, when your children are young or your job is very demanding, that you can do very little; at other times in your family, personal, and work life, you may have more time to participate in the community. Part of being successful is establishing realistic expectations about what you can and cannot accomplish with your finite amount of time and energy.

Turn saying "no" into an opportunity to do something for another person and to strengthen your reputation as someone who makes connections. Recommend someone else who could do the committee job or be the keynote speaker. This is an excellent way to provide growth opportunities for women you are mentoring or to make a referral to someone in your professional or personal network. It also expands the organization's network, creating new connections for it and generating additional support. Make the introductions. Both the person who has asked for your time and the person you recommend to fill the opportunity will see you as someone who makes things happen for others.

"When I was younger," says Maria Coyne, "I could do twelve things at one time, although none of them terribly good, but we all had this myth we could get everything done. With a little bit of age and wisdom, I finally realized that my time is worth something and I needed to scale back on the commitments to those that really are important to me."

You have just so much time and energy. Use it wisely.

Invest in Yourself: Your Intellectual, Physical, and Spiritual Well-being: In Summary

- Become a lifelong learner.
- Invest in wellness.
- Invest in your spirituality.
- Build personal support networks.
- Treat your time and energy as scarce and valuable resources.

Create Personal Wealth to Give Yourself the Life You Want

Most highly successful women view wealth not as a measure of success but as a resource to achieve their goals. Women value creating personal wealth because it allows them to have a comfortable life style, provide for their families, do things they enjoy, and be active philanthropists.

Men and women approach building wealth differently. "Men tend to be more quantitative. They tend to say, 'I want to have a certain amount of money and retire in this year in order to generate a certain amount of amount of income afterwards.' Women tend to be a little more fluid in their goals in terms of saying, 'I want to be able to do these things and then we have to come back and quantify them,'" says Diahann Lassus.

Develop and Implement a Plan for Creating Personal Wealth

As with business success, personal wealth creation requires determining what your definition of success is, setting high goals, understanding financial strategies and measurements, and evaluating and refining your strategy based on your progress.

Define what level of personal wealth you want to acquire. Once you have done this, develop a plan describing your personal goals and set specific, measurable financial objectives.

Involve Experts and Build Your Team

As you begin your planning process, a financial planner can be valuable to help you sift through all of the issues involved in developing your plan and bringing them together into a picture that helps you understand what you need to consider. At a minimum, you will have to deal with issues of cash flow, taxes, estate planning, and investment strategies. Depending on your personal situation, you may be adding a number of other issues to that list. If you have children or grandchildren, for example, the issue of education planning or generation-skipping trusts may be a priority for you.

By using an expert to help identify your needs, you will be able to work through your choices and develop your strategy. You will also learn what advisors you will need on your team to give you advice and provide services as you implement your plan. Understanding the level of expertise you will need for taxes, estate planning, insurance, and other subjects pertinent to your personal situation is imperative so that you make sure you have the level of sophistication you need. Seek input from other women about which advisors have met their needs and choose your team carefully.

Once you have developed your financial strategy, you can choose to do your own investing or hire someone to do it for you. If you feel qualified to do the investing yourself, be sure you consider the time it will take before you commit to doing it yourself. Building your personal financial wealth is too high a priority for it not to be done with sufficient resources. If you choose to have a professional do your investing, be strategic and thoughtful in selecting your team.

High-net-worth women (those with five million dollars or more in investable assets) need to take great care in selecting financial advisors. This is a time when one size does not fit all. Your relationship with your financial advisor is highly personal. These women say you need to know the qualifications of your advisor, understand how the advisor is compensated, and be comfortable that the advisor is acting in your best interests.[5] Most of these women talk with their advisors regularly, at least once a month.

Understand how you want your money invested. Many women choose to reflect their values in their choice of investments. They avoid investing in companies whose business practices or products are not consistent with their values. Laura, for instance, does not invest in tobacco companies because of her lifelong work in improving health.

Women are successful as investors. Research shows that women approach investing differently from men. The most successful women investors in these studies focus on long-term security. They tend to hold on to investments, trading 47 percent less frequently than men. Women emphasize a balanced portfolio and are less likely than men to invest on a tip or fad.[6] Women take the time to discuss their strategies with their advisors and expect the advisors to offer them solutions, not tell them what to do. The result, according to several studies, is that over the long term, the portfolios of women investors outperformed the portfolios of men investors and, in one study, even outperformed the market.[7] Women often enjoy working with other women on investments. Some join women investment clubs or invest through women angel networks.

According to Diahann Lassus, "Women tend to have goals that are more focused on future generations, perhaps planning to leave money for their kids. They are also focused on making sure they have enough money to support themselves well into their nineties." For women just moving into the business world, their life expectations may be past 100 years, so they need to plan for an even longer life.

Understand the Differences between High Income and High Net Worth, and Be Both

As women begin their careers, their personal financial attention is primarily focused on their salaries, what they make a year, and what standard of living they can have as a result. For most women, their salary provides the source of the dollars for savings and investments. In building personal wealth, the ultimate goal is to build a high net worth so you can have income beyond your salary and beyond your working years.

High income provides the resources to become high net worth. The better your compensation package, the easier it will be to achieve your goals. Each time your salary increases, set aside a portion of the increase for your investments and your savings.

Look beyond salary as compensation. Consider negotiating for an equity position. As you move into senior management, more options, including stock options, become available to you. There are consultants and attorneys who are compensation specialists and work with employees across many industries. They can be very helpful in advising you about what compensation package you can seek.

Take Advantage of Benefits Offered by Your Employer

Take full advantage of all of the benefits your company offers. Many companies offer benefits including 401(k) accounts, medical insurance, life insurance, disability insurance, and long-term care insurance. Take advantage of these benefits, as they are usually less expensive when bought through your company, as it has a broader risk pool and most companies contribute at least a portion of the cost.

Make creating personal wealth a personal strategy and a high priority as early in your career as possible. This will enable you to develop the financial wealth to live a full and comfortable life, provide for your family, and support the causes that are important to you.

Create Personal Wealth to Give Yourself the Life You Want: In Summary

- Develop and implement a plan for creating personal wealth.
- Involve experts and build your team.
- Understand the differences between high income and high net worth, and achieve both.
- Take advantage of the benefits offered by your employer.

Turn Possibilities into Reality

The journey has to be fun or it's not worth all the energy, time, and intellectual capital you pour into it. Success Strategy Eight is about having fun, reaching back to bring other women along with you, giving back to your community, and, most of all, being open to all that life brings your way.

Women Reaching Up and Reaching Back

"Women reaching up and reaching back" is imprinted on a T-shirt Sharon bought at a businesswomen's conference some years ago. A 12-year-old girl had a booth at the conference to sell T-shirts to raise money for a local charity. The young girl had designed the T-shirts and created the message printed on them by herself. Even at the age of 12, this young woman understood that energy shared is energy renewed and expanded. Share the experience, knowledge, and insights you have gained along the way—and the things you know now that you wish someone had told you earlier—with young women and men on their way up. The experience of expanding others' horizons expands your own horizons as well, so in giving back, you also enrich yourself. Begin reaching back as early as possible.

The days are over when highly successful women avoided being associated with women's organizations and causes, and shied away from helping other women for fear that if the women they helped did not perform well, it would reflect poorly on them. One of the honorees at an awards' conference of high-level women executives admitted to being one of those who distanced herself from other women for many years. She said, "Fortunately, I grew up and started helping other women."

Today, successful women take pride in mentoring both women and men. They believe they have a special responsibility to help other women in the workplace, in their industry, and in the community. Nina McLemore says that once a woman achieves success, she has a responsibility to help shine a light for other women. "Our mission as women is to create a world where women have a sense of their self-worth, ability to achieve, the opportunity to reach any goal they wish, and most importantly to have economic independence in order to make the best choices for themselves and their families," says Nina. She quotes Madeleine Albright, the first U.S. woman secretary of state: "There is a special place in hell for women who do not help each other."

Shining a light takes many forms. Start by being a role model for other women. "You can't be what you can't see," wrote one respondent in the Committee of 200 survey. When you are success-ful, even in your early career stages, other women will look to you as an example of how women lead. As you advance in the business world, the way you manage, the values you exhibit, and the way you treat others—colleagues, bosses, and, most of all, people who are junior to you—become a standard against which other women evalu-ate their own leadership styles and behavior. Furthermore, you not only influence other women. Increasingly we hear young men saying that they are influenced by the model set by women leaders in their organization.

Being a confident leader is the foundation for your legacy. Sharon Allen, former Chairman of the Board at Deloitte LLP, says you have to think about your legacy throughout your career, not just at the end.

Your legacy goes beyond a job title and official responsibilities. It is how you do things—the way you treat others and the way you reach out to help others throughout your career. What is important, says Sharon, is not what you are known *as*, but what you are known *for*.[1]

When you are successful, you open doors for other women. Marilyn Johnson says one of her key responsibilities is paving the way for other women. "I wanted to get ahead and do a good job so that when my name came up, people would say 'let's see what experience she brings us,' not 'let's take a risk,'" says Marilyn. "It was very important to me to do a good job so the white male managers would realize they weren't taking a risk when a woman or a woman of color came up for a position."

Be an Advocate for Women in Your Company

As you move into leadership roles, you have the opportunity to help your company capture the full value of women as part of its workforce. You understand better than your men colleagues the barriers holding women back from making their greatest contribution to the company. These are issues men leaders may not be aware of or fully comprehend. So when decisions about policies, promotions, or programs are being considered, the company's senior leadership team values the added, unique, and important perspective you can bring about how decisions may impact women—both positively and negatively.

Be an advocate for strategies that help retain women and give them the opportunity to make a contribution to the company's success, such as telecommuting and flexible work schedules. Make the business case for these strategies and remind everyone that these strategies are not only valued by women. While men are less likely to initiate a request for these work-life policies, when they are available, men appreciate and use them. For example, after Deloitte LLP—one of the pioneers in instituting initiatives to attract, retain, and promote women along the partnership track—introduced some of its signature programs intended for the women's initiative, men leaders asked that the initiatives be extended to include them. The result was higher morale and commitment to the company for both high-potential men and women.

Take the initiative to dispel generalizations such as the one that women do not want jobs requiring travel or relocation. Remind everyone that women and men are much alike in this respect; some are comfortable traveling or relocating and some are not. The best policy is to ask.

Encourage ongoing reviews of areas where research has found that despite policies intended to ensure equity between women and men, we still see disparities. A key area that should be reviewed regularly is compensation, starting with entry-level positions as part of the company's hiring and salary administration strategies.

Be Part of the Solution

Be proactive in bringing women into the business and helping them advance. Take the initiative when you are hiring from the outside to seek and recruit qualified women. Look for opportunities to promote women into senior positions.

Marilyn Johnson says part of the reason she wanted to become a vice president was because vice presidents select directors, and she wanted to be in a position to help women get into the executive positions. "I am not so much interested in women looking at my achievements and wanting to do the same. I want them to see they can roll on past me and go a lot further."

When opportunities open up, nominate women to be on the short list for consideration and encourage your men colleagues to do the same. Advocate for the women you know and respect.

Encourage senior managers to mentor and, most important, sponsor women leaders. Make connections between senior managers and high-potential women in the business.

If your company has a women's network, join and actively participate. If your company does not, start one. These networks give women opportunities to interact with and learn from other women across the company, at all levels of leadership, as well as with men corporate leaders. The networks provide an opportunity for women to discuss issues and get advice, and provide both formal and informal mentoring.

Increasingly, many companies also are using these women's networks to create connections between their women leaders and like-minded women clients. For example, GE's annual Leading and Learning Summit brings together top-level women from the company, customers, and the community. It has become a signature event, providing career-enhancing learning and connections. At Deloitte LLP, the women's network recently undertook a project to study women buyers and developed a training program on marketing to women for the men in the company. The training is being well received as a significant contribution to the business.

Mentor Women to Become Leaders
Think about the difference having mentors made to you and, in turn, make the same difference in the lives of other women. You are not only paying back what others have given to you, you are paying back the company that has given you the opportunity to be successful.

Mentoring can be as formal or informal as you wish. Sometimes other women will seek you out to be one of their mentors; in other cases, you may take the initiative to coach and offer advice to less experienced women within your business area or across the business. Educate them about the business and their role in the business. Provide informal coaching. Men managers, mentors, and sponsors usually are not comfortable discussing issues such as dress or mannerisms with women, so fill in the gaps on these subjects. Everyone—both the women and the men—will be grateful to you for taking on these issues.

Most important, give the women you mentor insight into what it takes to get ahead in business and in your company specifically. Share advice on how best to build internal relationships and sponsorships. Schedule lunch or coffee every so often to answer questions, listen to their ideas, and provide leadership tips. In addition to your own informal mentoring, be an advocate for establishing formal mentoring programs for women within the company and participate.

The professional networks and associations you have developed to enhance your career also provide opportunities for you to mentor and support women in your industry or community. Again, mentoring does not have to take a great deal of time—an occasional informal meeting, a brief telephone call when your mentee needs advice, or an exchange of e-mails often provides just the support the woman needs. Encourage your professional associations to establish formal mentoring programs for women that, in addition to one-on-one mentoring, include events to provide business and industry education, insights from women leaders, and networking.

Bring Women into Professional Organizations
Look at the makeup of your professional organizations. Is there a critical mass of women members? If not, reach out to other women who would benefit from the organizations. Invite them to events and receptions, and when they come, take them around to meet people. Encourage women to become members, welcome them once they join, and help them focus on the opportunities offered by committees or activities where they can be visible and gain experience.

Be a Role Model in the Community at Large

We discussed being visible in the media as part of creating your personal brand. The same principles apply to being a role model for women inside your company and in the community at large.

Be Visible in the Media
Print and web-based publications are always seeking successful women to interview for stories on "how they made it." As you move ahead in business, it also is an opportunity to provide knowledge and inspiration to other women. The media magnifies your impact by reaching a much broader audience than one-on-one mentoring and in-person meetings. The interview questions usually focus on your experiences, challenges, leadership style, and advice for other women. As we cautioned in using media for personal branding, be sure to check in with your company's public relations department for guidance.

Be Active in the Community

If you belong to a women's organization, the group may have formal programs to reach out to women students, provide internships, or sponsor events where leading women speak and share their experiences. This is an excellent way to inspire young women to dream big and be open to the possibilities.

As your schedule permits, accept or even seek out opportunities to speak to women's groups, share your insights, and be a role model. Choose the opportunities based on your values, strategies, and goals. Don't forget to consider how these commitments fit in with your schedule priorities. Often you can combine professional and personal priorities by bringing your company in as a sponsor for these organizations. The organization, your company, and you benefit from such sponsorships. The sponsorship will strengthen the nonprofit organization, expand your contribution to the nonprofit's success, and give you a reputation within your company for identifying opportunities to extend the company's marketing or public relations outreach.

For example, Monica Luechtefeld has identified specific women's organizations to support consistent with her company's professional and her personal priorities. She attends their conferences and speaks on panels to share her business expertise and experience. Through company sponsorships, she is able to expand the resources available to the organizations and make a difference in the opportunities for the women members. Additionally, this has enabled her company to become a leader in its support of small business entrepreneurs and women business owners in particular.

Be a Sponsor for Women

Every woman who is in a position to be a sponsor should sponsor women as well as men. Gaining sponsors is one of the last barriers for women still to be torn down. Seek out high-performing women and get to know them. Give them opportunities to work with you or other leaders on high-profile projects. Introduce them to other leaders, especially men, and encourage the men to become advocates for the women. Become known as someone who knows the best and the brightest women and can bring them to the table, whether in your company, the community, your industry, or professional associations. This enhances your reputation as well as opening up opportunities for other women.

Educate the Future Leaders

Your role in supporting other women goes beyond the simple sum of all these specific actions. Women are the educators for both women and men within the workplace, the community, and for future generations.

"Our obligation as women is to ensure that our sons and daughters and the generation of children they are raising have a very different view of women and their potential in the workforce and contribution in society and the community," says Monica. "We have the responsibility to give back not only at work but in our families, homes, and communities."

"I worried about the lesson my son was taking away from me as a mom," continues Monica. "When I asked, he told me it was two things: first was that the family is the most important thing, and they are there for you regardless of what happens; and second was the belief that he could be anything he wanted to be, that he had unlimited possibilities. When I heard that, I knew I had done my job!"

Women Reaching Up and Reaching Back: In Summary

- Be an advocate for women in your company.
- Be part of the solution.
- Mentor women to become leaders.
- Bring women into professional organizations.
- Be a role model in the community at large.
- Be visible in the media.
- Be active in the community.

- Be a sponsor for women.
- Educate the future leaders.

The Power of Philanthropy

When women are successful, they want to share their success by helping others and being a force for positive change. Every woman can harness the power of philanthropy to create the changes she wants to see. "I think it's important for each of us personally to recognize that we can make a difference through philanthropy," says Diahann Lassus.

Women traditionally have been the backbone of community philanthropy, and today's successful women are no different. They give close to twice as much as men at almost every income level,[2] and are more likely to volunteer in leadership positions in the organizations they support.[3]

You do not have to wait until you are making a lot of money. Make the practice of philanthropy part of your life as early as possible. Contribute personally significant gifts every year. A personally significant gift is one that you can afford based on your current financial situation. As your career progresses, you can increase your monetary contributions as your personal financial position flourishes. Women of achievement make substantial financial gifts to the organizations and projects they support—but most started with small annual contributions.

Practice Strategic Philanthropy
to Make the Greatest Difference

Be focused and strategic in your giving. You will have a greater impact by concentrating your contributions on several key causes and organizations that are important to you than by scattering small contributions to every worthwhile organization.

Select the causes and organizations you will support based on your vision and passions. In general, women give to causes that are important to them personally, to give back to the community or organizations that supported them as they were building their professional and personal lives, and to make a better future for others.[4] In some cases, your contribution will be primarily financial; in others, you may wish to commit personal time as well as money. Diahann Lassus makes her philanthropic decisions based on three criteria. "For me, it is about those things I believe in, like cancer research and suicide prevention, those I enjoy, like my Florida State ladies basketball team, and those where I believe I can really make a difference by committing my personal time as well as money, like organizations focused on women's entrepreneurship."

Look for opportunities to give where you can make the greatest impact. For example, you can make a greater impact with the same amount of money by supporting smaller organizations. One woman told us she realized her contribution at the large university where she received her undergraduate education would not make much difference because they have such a large base of givers. So she decided to focus her philanthropy on a smaller college where her contribution would make a real difference in the number of scholarships available to students. In addition, by focusing your philanthropy on a smaller organization, you have the opportunity to personally influence strategy and the success of the organization.

In addition to the significance of the cause to you, if you are like most women, you want to know the nonprofits you support are well run. You can check out the nonprofit's financial statements and the annual report. Look at the sources of the organization's funding. Review the programming and ask how the activities make a difference in the community. Look at the list of contributors. Do you see friends or colleagues whose judgments you trust and whom you can ask about the organization? Are these people with whom you want to be affiliated? You can also attend a couple of events and meet other stakeholders.

Be financially strategic in how you structure your giving. In the United States, the tax code favors charitable giving. As your philanthropic capacity increases, you should consult a financial advisor about the various vehicles for philanthropy to reduce your tax liability, increase the benefit of your gift to the nonprofit, and continue to care for your family. Planning for philanthropy should be integral to your personal wealth management strategy.

You Can Give Money without Giving Time

When you are approached for a contribution, your first reaction may be, "I just don't have the time to participate in another organization." So you say you cannot contribute. When women believe in a cause, they want to make a substantial impact by committing time as well as their money. However, your ability to be personally involved will vary over the course of time, depending on what is going on in the various parts of your life. (Remember, you are setting priorities.) As much as you would like to be active in the organization, this may not be the time.

However, if it is an organization you believe is worthwhile and one you would like to support, demonstrate your commitment by writing the check. Your financial support will contribute to the organization's ability to continue its good work. Continue to be a supporter. Follow the organization through its publications and attend occasional events. When your priorities permit, become active. Having been a supporter for a period of time will make you a more effective volunteer leader because you already understand the organization's mission, program priorities, and culture.

Multiply the Impact of Your Philanthropy

You can multiple your impact on behalf of the causes and organizations you support by bringing financial resources from your company. If your company has a matching funds program, be certain to apply on behalf of the nonprofit. Identify opportunities for company support through the company's formal philanthropic programs or grants from the company foundation. Help the leaders of nonprofit organizations you support structure opportunities that are attractive to your business and aligned with your company's philanthropic strategies. Then help shepherd the nonprofit organization leaders through the process. Make introductions to the right people for the nonprofit and be an advocate for the nonprofit within your company.

You may be able to offer to host meetings on-site in your company or provide products or services to the nonprofit organization. This becomes an opportunity for the nonprofit to benefit from your company's expertise and for your company to gain valuable visibility with the nonprofit's members and supporters. Many times the organizations you support, especially the women's organizations, represent markets for your company, and you can facilitate sponsorships using marketing dollars.

Philanthropy often ties in with your professional aspirations. If you are passionate about your profession, you are likely to be passionate about causes related to your profession and therefore your career. Bring your professional connections to the nonprofit organization and your nonprofit connections to the business. Make introductions and connections between the nonprofit leaders and leaders in your company and your industry associations. This is another way to be viewed as a connector by your company, within the community, and in your professional associations as well as making a substantial contribution to the nonprofit.

Serve on Nonprofit Boards

Once you become active in the organization as a volunteer or contributor, you are likely to receive an invitation to serve on the board of directors. Serving on the board is an opportunity to expand your impact and influence on the organization and to make a difference. It can be an exhilarating experience, an opportunity to expand and diversify your professional networks and make new friends. Serving on nonprofit boards also provides experience and expertise in collegial decision making, a factor many corporate board leaders take into consideration when selecting new board members.

Do your due diligence when you are invited to join an organization's board. Look at the other members of the board of directors. Ask about the level of commitment required:

- Number of meetings a year
- Where the meetings are held

- Required financial contribution
- Expected involvement on committees

Review the latest financial statements and audit reports as well as the past annual reports. Remember, when you join a board of directors, you have fiduciary responsibility for the organization.

Share the Power of Philanthropy with Other Women

Bring other women along with you on your philanthropic journey. Encourage them to give to organizations important to them. Introduce them to the nonprofits you support by taking them to an event or introducing them to nonprofit leaders. As part of your mentoring, include the importance of women giving back and help your mentees identify how and where they want to make a difference.

In addition to giving as an individual, you may want to expand the impact of your philanthropy by creating or joining a giving circle. Giving circles bring together a group of women to support a cause or event. While each person's contribution may be relatively small, when the group pools its contributions, they make a substantial difference. Some giving circles are informal, with a small number of members who meet and select the charities they will support. Other giving circles are much larger organizations, with officers and formal policies to guide their selection of the causes and organizations they will support. Giving circles are an effective way to extend the impact of your contributions, especially when you are just beginning your career and philanthropy.

Many areas now have women's foundations. In general, these foundations aggregate the contributions of multiple givers to provide grants to local organizations that help women. Like giving circles, this is a way to increase the impact of your contribution.

Make Philanthropy a Family Value

Instill the value of giving in your children and make philanthropy a family affair. Laura always placed a high priority on her children understanding that whether or not they had much money, they were very blessed and had a responsibility to help others. Every year at Thanksgiving, the children chose a charitable cause to support. The tradition of giving as a family continues, and, as adults, they come together once a year to talk about their philanthropic priorities and the causes the family will support in the coming year.

The Power of Philanthropy: In Summary

- Use the power of philanthropy to create the change you want to see.
  - Practice strategic philanthropy to make the greatest difference.
  - You can give money without giving time.
  - Multiply the impact of your philanthropy.
- Serve on nonprofit boards.
- Share the power of philanthropy with other women.
- Make philanthropy a family value.

Be Open to Serendipity

Serendipity is the magical word used by Mary Poppins to describe the joys and opportunities that appear unexpectedly in life. Mary Poppins told the children to believe that the impossible can be possible. If you take away nothing else from this book, we hope you realize that you can make anything you want come true once you figure out how to approach the journey.

Life is a lot like a kaleidoscope. Each time you rotate the kaleidoscope, even a little, the bits of glass shift to form a new overall image. You see new colors and shapes and possibilities as the same pieces come together in different and unexpected ways. Keep rotating your view of life and discover all the exhilarating new possibilities and potential.

Consciously open up your schedule to allow time to think, muse, and explore. Think about your life and career. Reflect on the possibilities. Stretch beyond what you are doing today. Listen to what others say about what you could do or could be. Consider "what if." Be alert to new opportunities, especially if they do not fit with your preconceptions of what you want. Rotate your kaleidoscope and discover how the pieces fit together to form a new picture. Give yourself the freedom to experiment.

"You need to allow time for opportunity to present itself. If you are so tied into your own world and set in all the things you do, a really great opportunity might just walk right by you and you wouldn't have time to take advantage of it," reflects Kathe Albrecht. "Part of serendipity is that there is serendipity. Serendipity definitely occurs, but if you are so focused that you can't slow down to recognize it, then you are at a big disadvantage."

Sometimes opportunities arise as the result of your personal reflections, insights, and imagination. Sometimes they will come from the outside. Life presents you with possibilities you never imagined. These may be small things that bring you great enjoyment or major opportunities that open up a whole new world for you.

In your career, serendipity often occurs in the form of positions or projects you would never know about or might never have chosen for yourself. These often turn out to be the best learning experiences and may launch your career in a totally different and more rewarding direction. Maria Coyne says some of the assignments that provided her the best career opportunities were totally unexpected. "Serendipity really means to be flexible and open to new things you did not originally think were a part of the plan and to be willing to go down that path and see what you can learn from it," says Maria.

Serendipity in business means staying nimble. Devote time to thinking strategically about your business. Camye Mackey includes time to think in her schedule. "We are constantly on the go, but scheduling time to think is important—time to process what is happening. I think about the meetings I have had, the people I've met with, and what they said. I need the time to think about how I can use this knowledge for the betterment of my job and the business," says Camye.

Business opportunities present themselves in some of the most unexpected times and from unexpected sources, for example:

- A friend refers a new client who doesn't fit your normal customer profile.
- A customer asks you to provide a service you had never considered.
- A colleague approaches you about collaborating on a new way of operating.

Beware of missing or dismissing these opportunities because you are so focused on your day-to-day plan. Be open to saying, "Yes, let's try it and see where it leads." The results may be the opportunity to create a new market ahead of your competition, design a new business offering, or build a more productive operation.

"Don't underestimate the role that happy accidents play in your personal life or your career," says Susan Helstab. "You need to be open to taking advantage of those unanticipated accidents when they come along. You can plan a life, but ultimately, it's the things you can't plan that have the biggest influence on your life."

Stay open to being spontaneous. Sometimes the best moments in life are those that pop up unexpectedly. On the spur of the moment ,you decide to take your child to see the holiday displays in department store windows. A friend calls and says, "Let's celebrate my promotion." You decide to give your team a special luncheon to recognize how hard they have been working. Seize these moments. They bring joy and meaning into your life.

Celebrate the Journey

We wrote this book because we believe every woman should dream big dreams and have the knowledge and tools to make her dreams a reality. We wanted to make the journey easier for you by giving you the benefit of the experiences and insights from women business leaders who have achieved high levels of success.

We want you to be successful because we strongly believe the business world will benefit when there are confident, visionary women like you in every level of leadership and in all parts of the business world.

Like a performing artist, now that you have mastered the basic techniques, you are free to improvise. You can customize your life to integrate family, professional, and personal priorities in your own way. You can make the journey anything you want it to be.

Celebrate the journey. Take pride in your accomplishments every day. Do the things that you love to do and that make you happy. Take time to learn, teach, lead, be led, and make a difference. Get to know fabulous people. Make friends. Enjoy your family. Have fun. You will find you have created a life that is your legacy.

Biographies

These biographies are of the phenomenal women who generously shared their experiences, insights, and advice. Their stories and comments illustrate and bring to life the eight essential strategies of successful women. Some of them we have known and been inspired by for many years. Others we met for the first time through writing this book. We stand in awe of every one of them. They truly represent all that women can be for each other, and we thank them for being an integral part of the adventure of writing this book.

KATHE HICKS ALBRECHT
Visual Resources Curator
American University

After graduating from the University of California, Los Angeles (UCLA) with a degree in art history, Kathe spent a semester in architecture school, but was discouraged by the lack of support for women in architecture at that time. After moving to Washington, D.C., she worked for a time in interior design and then earned a master's degree from American University in art history, specializing in architectural history. As a student, she worked in what was then called the Slide Library. When the Slide Library curator left on maternity leave, Kathe was offered the curator position. It was a field she had never considered, but she soon discovered that she loved it.

Because the field was in its infancy and in transition, Kathe had the opportunity to make it what she wanted. She guided the transition from analog to digital visual information and expanded the field's impact across the university and the industry. Kathe says, "There was a lot of opportunity, but I had to advocate for myself. I had many colleagues who wouldn't change with the move to digital and got left behind."

Today, Kathe is responsible for developing and maintaining an extensive digital image collection used for the art history classroom and other humanities disciplines. She trains and supervises the Visual Resources Center staff on all aspects of digital asset management and instructs faculty on the use of the department's image database and online digital resources. She is involved in running the graduate program in art history and is an informal student advisor.

Kathe has defined her leadership as going beyond the university to her industry. She has been involved in groundbreaking national initiatives on the use of digital information and its impact on the educational community, including a major Getty Foundation–funded grant for a national pilot program that studied museum image use in universities. She has published broadly on the educational use of digital images, including the analog to digital transition, educational fair use, and copyright.

Kathe cochaired the committee that managed American University's participation in the Museum Educational Site Licensing Project, a national initiative to explore the academic use of licensed museum images and information. She also served on the U.S. government's Conference on Fair Use (CONFU) in the area of digital image use. Recently, her work has focused on exploring aspects of the 21st-century learning space, examining ways of learning that best accommodate "digital natives," the youth of today. At the time we interviewed her, she was launching her latest project, the first annual Feminist Art History Conference, an American University–sponsored event, that drew leaders and scholars from around the world.

Kathe is a recognized leader in her professional association, the Visual Resources Association (VRA). She has served as VRA president, and now sits on the board of directors of the Visual Resources Association Foundation, VRA's educational and research enterprise.

Kathe is married and has three children.

MARIA C. COYNE
Executive Vice President, Consumer and
Small Business Segment Head, KeyBank
Member, Executive Council at KeyCorp

Maria Coyne graduated from the University of Notre Dame with a degree in business finance. She completed the Key Executive Experience training program at Case Western Reserve University's Weatherhead School of Management.

Maria says she always wanted to be a banker, and, with the exception of three years at a nonprofit economic development organization, she has been working in banking her whole career. Shortly out of college, she joined Bank One in Cleveland, Ohio, where she worked for 10 years. She served in various management capacities, ultimately becoming director of marketing. She moved to the Greater Cleveland Growth Association, where she spent three years as a small business strategist. In 2001, she joined KeyBank as a senior vice president in the strategic planning group.

At KeyBank, her positions have included Chief Administrative Officer for Key Community Banking and Director of Client Experience and Business Banking Segment Head. Maria was an early believer in the importance of women-owned businesses as a high-growth emerging market and was the founder of the Key4Women program for women business owners. This program provides financial solutions, networking, and education for women business owners. Today, as Executive Vice President and Consumer and Small Business Segment Head, she continues to be responsible for KeyBank's Key4Women program.

Maria is a sought-after speaker on small business topics and has been featured on CNN, SmartMoney.com, and National Public Radio (NPR), as well in national publications including the *Wall Street Journal*, *Enterprising Women*, *BusinessWeek SmallBiz*, *American Banker*, and *U.S. Banker*.

Maria's commitment to the advancement of women-owned businesses is reflected in her board memberships, which include the Advisory Council of the Center for Women's Business Research, the board of directors of Women Presidents' Organization, and the Forbes Executive Women Board. In Cleveland, Maria is a member of the MacDonald

Women's Health Leadership Council and the Finance Committee for the Cleveland Catholic Diocese.

Maria is married with two children. For over a decade she has served on the board of directors for the high school that both she and her daughter attended; in addition, she served as chairperson for four years. She believes that being involved in the community helps keep her grounded and focused on what's important.

DEBRA HANNA
Associate Director, Critical Path to TB Drug Consortium, Critical Path Institute former Senior Principal Scientist, Laboratory Head, and Project Team Leader for Antibacterial Research, Pfizer Worldwide Research & Development

Debra Hanna received her undergraduate degree from Colorado State University and received her Ph.D. in microbiology from North Carolina State University. She did postgraduate work at the University of California, San Diego, where she became involved in research focused on infectious diseases for underserved populations, which became her passion. While she was completing her postdoctoral research, Debra had time to reflect on whether she wanted to pursue an academic route or go into for-profit business. Because her goal was to design and develop new medicines for underserved patients, she decided the pharmaceutical industry was the right path for her.

Debra joined Pfizer as the Lead Scientist in its antibiotic drug discovery and development unit in Ann Arbor, Michigan. She was a Project Team Leader for multiple drug discovery and development programs, as well as Laboratory Head for 10 years within the Antibacterial Research Unit at Pfizer Worldwide Research & Development.

When the Ann Arbor Research & Development facilities were closed, Debra relocated to Groton, Connecticut, to work in the Antibacterials unit. The company wanted to change the culture and thinking at the Groton lab, so she was brought in as both a scientific leader and a change agent. After about five years, the decision was made to transfer the research unit's mission office to China. Debra traveled to China and was involved in developing the transition and hiring strategy for the research unit.

This move happened at a time when Debra already had begun to realize she was going to have to move either outside her role in the Antibacterials unit to another position in Pfizer or move externally in order to advance. Further, she realized she wanted to get closer to her passion of treating diseases affecting underserved populations and neglected diseases. When the lab transfer was announced, she had already started her exploration.

Now, Debra accelerated her search outside Pfizer. She had been working with Critical Path Institute as a Pfizer representative on a large tuberculosis effort they had been leading. The position she now holds actually became available the week after Pfizer announced the move of her unit to China. Through her networks, she interviewed very quickly. She decided it was the right fit because it aligned with her values, her scientific expertise, and her passion for underserved patients. In addition, the position was in Tucson, Arizona, which was in line with her personal goals as well. Debra is originally from Colorado and had hopes of fulfilling her professional aspirations as well as being closer to her family. She had a strong interest in serving on a nonprofit board for a community organization and Tucson represented a community with opportunities.

While at Pfizer, Debra led the Women's Leadership Network, supporting over 900 women from entry levels to executive titles. In 2010, she received the "Leading Women to the Top™ IWiN" award, honoring extraordinary commitment and leadership by an individual woman. This award, presented by the Leading Women Organization, recognized Debra for being a champion of women's professional development and career advancement within her organization and its internal women's network. Although she now lives in Tucson, she has continued her mentor/mentee relationships with this organization.

Debra is a single mother with one child.

SUSAN HELSTAB
Executive Vice President, Marketing,
Four Seasons Hotels and Resorts

Susan Helstab grew up working in her family's business, where her primary responsibility was helping with the bookkeeping. Since she did not particularly enjoy bookkeeping, she felt certain she would never go into business. Inspired by her high school biology teacher, she decided to major in biology when she went to university. She graduated with honors from the University of Toronto and planned to teach biology.

However, there were no openings for biology teachers when she graduated, so she decided to work for a year while figuring out what to do with her life. It took only three months to decide she desperately wanted to get back into the academic world. It didn't matter what she studied; she just wanted to return to school as quickly as possible. She chose business school because there was a program she could start immediately. Susan fell in love with business almost immediately and earned her master of business administration degree from York University, with a dual major in finance and marketing. The dual major opened up a wide range of opportunities for her, from banking to marketing of consumer packaged goods.

At that time, Susan's criteria for evaluating the companies she interviewed with was whether they would be fun places to work. Advertising attracted her because it was interesting and creative, and she accepted a position with McCann-Erickson Advertising. She loved advertising and spent eight years at the firm, advancing to vice president. She worked in the advertising agency's offices in New York and Toronto in progressively higher positions of responsibility in account management. Her diverse account responsibilities included major brands such as Coca-Cola, American Express, Nescafé, Johnson & Johnson, and Tetley Tea.

When Four Seasons Hotels and Resorts approached Susan to join the company doing advertising and promotion, she was intrigued. Being in the travel and hospitality industry was attractive to her, since she had traveled extensively as a child with her family and traveling continued to be one of her aspirations. The company was very well respected in the community and had a reputation as a great employer. In addition, it would be an opportunity to work with the company's founder, Isadore Sharp, who was a business icon. So Susan joined Four Seasons in 1987.

In 2009 Susan was named Executive Vice President of Marketing. In this position, she oversees a global sales and marketing organization that includes reservations, direct sales, advertising, promotion, public relations, and direct marketing, as well as the brand's online presence through social media and its website, and the Four Seasons print and online magazines.

Susan currently serves on the Advisory Council of Sunnybrook Health Sciences Foundation; is a member of the U.S. Travel Association's Meetings, Incentives and Trade Show Council (MIT); and is on the advisory board of the Cornell Center for Hospitality Research at Cornell University. Susan is married and has one child.

BEVERLY A. HOLMES
Founder and CEO, B. A. Holmes & Associates
Retired, Senior Vice President, Retirement Services
Division, MassMutual Financial Group

Beverly Holmes graduated from Southern New Hampshire University, Manchester with a degree in human services. She received her master's degree in education from Cambridge College. While she was looking for a position in the field of human services after college, a family friend offered, and she accepted, a sales position in a financial services company selling annuities, life insurance, and mutual funds. Into her second year, she realized that although the work was not in the field of human services, it was challenging (financial services sales was a tough job for a woman, especially for a woman of color in the early 1980s), but it also was professionally rewarding.

Beverly discovered that she liked what she was doing in financial services, but she needed to work where the compensation was predictable. To fulfill this desire, she went to work for a consulting firm that provided business management services to radiologists. In this role, she became a member of a team that provided retirement planning and advice to the doctors and their staff. This was her first introduction to the field of retirement services. She remembers saying to herself, "This is it, this is what I want to do; this is the area where I want to specialize." She had found her passion in an elite little niche of the financial services industry.

While Beverly enjoyed the consulting work and the encouragement and support of her boss (really her first great mentor), she recognized she needed to know more about the business from a provider perspective. This started her on a journey to develop the skills she needed to become a successful contributor in her new field. She had gained experience working with, and on behalf of, customers; she was now ready to focus on the other side of the business, which meant she needed to work for a company that provided retirement products and services.

Beverly's pursuit led her to Aetna (today ING) in Hartford, Connecticut. There she further refined her professional and technical skills, devoting her time to retirement product development, marketing, and sales support. After four years, she decided it was time to take all that she had learned from the customers and the service provider and leverage her retirement services background. Her focus was to find a company that would allow her to work in a sales operation, educating financial advisors on products and services and how to use these tools to sell retirement plans to business owners. So with her experience and accomplishments in hand, she pursued and found the perfect position at MassMutual Financial Group, a premier retirement services provider. This is where she spent the remainder of her career.

The move to MassMutual presented an opportunity for Beverly to accomplish a long-held desire and goal: she wanted and believed it was possible for a woman and a woman of color to create, develop, and grow a profitable business by providing 401(k) retirement plans to small businesses through third party distributors. After a number of years of operational successes and developing relationships with distributors of retirement plans, products, and services, she was able to convince her executive vice president that she could bring new customers and new assets to the company by taking a bold step to enter a new market segment.

Under Beverly's leadership and management, her new business developed and grew to $4 billion in assets under management. Her achievement gained her notoriety inside and outside the company, and she was recognized with the company's prestigious "President's Leadership Award." Today, this business entity continues as a viable operation for the company.

While working in the financial services field, Beverly developed a keen sense of the financial needs of women. Her passion for economic development and retirement security for women prompted many of her advocacy activities. She has traveled nationally and internationally, speaking and advising on economic and retirement security opportunities for women.

Beverly's volunteer work has complemented her business and advocacy commitments. She serves on the board of Women's Institute for a Secure Retirement (WISER), was chair of the board of directors for the Center for Women's Business Research, and was a member of the board of directors at Bay Path College.

After joining MassMutual, Beverly established a personal retirement goal: retire from the company healthy and prosperous to do the things she enjoys. She achieved her goal when she retired in January 2010. Her retirement life is as full as her professional life. She was appointed by the Massachusetts governor to the Massachusetts Board of Elementary and Secondary Education and was elected vice chair of the board in 2011. She is founder and CEO of B. A. Holmes & Associates, which provides leadership development coaching and consulting services for personal and business growth. She also coauthored the book *Applied Leadership: Putting Theory into Practice.*

Beverly has a married daughter who is a successful professional with Microsoft.

MARILYN JOHNSON
Retired, Vice President, Market Development, IBM

Marilyn Johnson received her undergraduate degree from John Marshall University in Huntington, West Virginia, and completed two master's degrees in education. She began her career teaching in the public school system. She also worked as a broadcaster for a local NBC affiliate television station.

At IBM, Marilyn started out as a Market Support Systems Engineer. She has held positions with both U.S. and worldwide responsibility, including Director of Financial Services Sector, Director of eBusiness Infrastructure, and Director of Worldwide Sales Operations. She also has held executive positions in key IBM business units and has had management and operational responsibility in North America, the Middle East, Africa, Latin America, and Asia. In 1999, she led the merger of IBM and Sequent Corporation Web-Server Sales.

As Vice President, Market Development, Marilyn led an organization responsible for developing IBM's strategy for marketing to businesses owned or operated by Asians, blacks, Hispanics, Native Americans, and women in the Americas. Her responsibilities also included worldwide responsibility for marketing to women-led and women-owned businesses.

She has served on the executive board of the Council of Better Business Bureaus; the executive boards of the Asian Pacific Islander American Scholarship Foundation, the National Council of Negro Women, and the American Airlines Marketing Advisory Council; and the advisory board for One World Theater in Austin, Texas. She was an active member of the Center for Women's Business Research Advisory Council, taking a lead role in issues concerning women entrepreneurs and technology. Within IBM, she was one of the founders and leaders of the first black diversity network.

Marilyn is actively involved in mentoring both within IBM and in the community. She currently has more than 21 mentees worldwide.

Marilyn has received numerous awards for her support of women and women of color, including being named one of "The Top 25 Influential Black Women" by *Network Journal Magazine*. Most recently, she was awarded the title of "Women's Global Champion" by the National Association of Female Executives.

Marilyn was married for 18 years. She has two children, whom she raised to graduate with honors from college, and one grandson. Marilyn recently retired and is looking forward to having time to adopt a puppy.

DIAHANN W. LASSUS, CFP®, CPA/PFS
President and Chief Investment Officer,
Lassus Wherley

Diahann Lassus earned her bachelor's degree in management at Florida State University. She received her master of business administration degree at the University of North Florida.

Diahann worked in accounting and line operations at Blue Cross Blue Shield, Xerox Corporation, and AT&T. She met her business partner, Clare Wherley, when they both worked for AT&T on the 1984 Summer Olympics in Los Angeles. Clare was the Project Manager, and Diahann was the Field Operations Manager. Diahann was responsible for the technical people setting up the telephone systems and terminals for the computers and worked with the volunteers who helped the athletes use the systems. She managed 700 people and worked 7 days a week, 20 hours a day for 9 months.

After this experience, coming back to a normal job was not attractive. Diahann and Clare decided to start their own company consulting with small businesses. But after Diahann saw an ad from the College for Financial Planning, they refocused the business on financial planning and accounting.

Diahann and Clare thought their market would be primarily small business owners, but the first client who walked through the door was a widow who needed personal financial planning help. The client referred her friends and colleagues, and the focus of the business soon shifted to individual financial planning. Today Lassus Wherley is one of the leading boutique wealth management firms, with offices in New Providence, New Jersey, and Bonita Springs, Florida.

Diahann and the firm have been recognized with multiple awards for excellence and leadership in financial planning. Diahann has been named seven times to *Worth* magazine's list of "Top Financial Advisors." The National Association of Personal Financial Advisors (NAPFA) presented her with the "2010 Robert J. Underwood Distinguished Service Award." The award recognizes a professional who has made a significant contribution to the advancement of the practice of fee-only financial planning and advising. In 2011 she was named one of the "Top 50 Women in Wealth" by AdvisorOne, recognizing her contributions and influence in the wealth management industry.

Diahann is a tireless advocate on behalf of financial literacy, especially for girls, and for strengthening the financial planning profession. She was the inaugural speaker for the Rothman Institute of Entrepreneurship's Female Entrepreneurship Series and participated as a speaker in the Charles A. Bruning Florida State University Distinguished Speaker's Series. Diahann and Clare were recently listed among the "Top 25 Leading Women Entrepreneurs" in New Jersey by Own It Ventures.

Diahann's high-profile appointments have included being appointed by President Bill Clinton to the Retirement Savings Summit in Washington, D.C. in 1998, and being appointed by New Jersey Governor Christie Todd Whitman to the New Sources of Capital Board in 1996. Diahann regularly testifies before Congress on issues affecting the financial planning profession.

Diahann currently serves on the Financial Planning Coalition as a representative for the National Association of Personal Financial Advisors and is a member of the board of directors of the New Jersey State Chamber of Commerce. She has also served on corporate and advisory boards, including Charles Schwab Institutional, Women's Financial Network at Siebert, NJN Professional Advisory Board, International Institute of NJ, and National Advisors Trust Company, FSB.

Diahann actively supports entrepreneurship and women's business ownership. She has served as President of the National Association of

Women Business Owners. Currently she serves on the board of directors for the Center for Women's Business Research and the Rothman Institute of Entrepreneurship Advisory Board.

MONICA LUECHTEFELD
Executive Vice President, E-Commerce, at Office Depot and former member, Executive Committee at Office Depot

Monica Luechtefeld graduated from Mount Saint Mary's College in Los Angeles, California, with a bachelor's degree in biological sciences and chemistry. She finished her degree requirements a semester early, and while waiting to graduate, she took a job in the college admissions office doing college relations and student recruiting. She enjoyed it so much that she decided to stay on after graduation working in college relations, ending up ultimately as Director of Admissions for the college. The role offered her a wonderful opportunity to engage students in a mentoring and coaching role, and the ability to have an impact on the education and future of young women.

However, the position demanded weekend and evening hours plus ongoing availability to parents and students. So when Monica decided to start a family, she made the difficult decision to leave. A close family friend had an office products and supply company and offered her a job. She took it, thinking it was an interim position until she was ready to return to management and leadership. After her son was born, she continued in outside sales, learning a great deal about juggling a young baby, keeping customers happy, and building a successful career. Several years later, the company was acquired by a larger office products company, Eastman. Monica moved into management and eventually became Vice President of Sales and then Vice President of the Office Furniture Division. This gave her experience in recruiting, training, and managing people in a sales organization, as well as experience in the back office operational functions required to keep a furniture dealership running.

It was a time of change and consolidation in the office supplies industry, and Monica, along with a group of Eastman leaders, had the idea that office supplies should move from a silo mentality, where a supplier either serves small business customers or has large contract business with corporate customers, into a consolidated model, where a supplier serves customers across the entire spectrum of size. They created a model for the office supply enterprise of the future. They pitched the concept to Office Depot, which led to Office Depot acquiring Eastman and putting Monica in charge of the integration of the two companies.

Office Depot made seven additional acquisitions. Monica became Vice President of Marketing and Sales Administration, which included leading the integration of the seven acquisitions. One of these acquired firms had a relationship with Massachusetts Institute of Technology (MIT), and Monica was invited to a presentation on an innovative idea—the Internet as a business tool. Convinced that the Internet was the future of business-to-business commerce and potentially of retailing, she became an advocate for e-commerce. Monica is credited with being the architect and advocate of the blueprint that ultimately made Office Depot number five in the prestigious Internet Retail Top 500 ranking; this transformed her career.

Throughout Monica's career at Office Depot, she has been in a pioneering role, creating new markets and new ways of serving those markets. Monica held senior and executive positions, continuing to expand and improve Office Depot's e-commerce footprint along with leading business units in information technology (IT), business development, and supply chain. She supported Office Depot's global expansion. She served as Executive Vice President of Global E-Commerce and Direct Marketing, with responsibility for delivering $4.1 billion in online revenue for Office Depot. Her responsibilities included driving innovation and customer-driven features and functionality across the company's web platforms.

Throughout her career, Monica also leveraged her numerous relationships with women's organizations to expand Office Depot's support to women professionals and women business owners. She served on the Department of Homeland Security's Private Sector Senior Advisory Committee, the board of directors of the Institute for Economic Empowerment of Women, the Florida International University's College of Business Advisory Board, and the board of trustees of Mount Saint Mary's College.

Monica currently is pursuing an advanced degree in business management. She holds an honorary doctorate from Mount Saint Mary's College.

Monica was a single mother and has a successful son, a talented daughter-in-law, and two beautiful grandchildren.

CAMYE MACKEY
Vice President of Human Resources
B. F. Saul Company Hospitality Group

Camye Mackey fell in love with the Washington, D.C., area on a family vacation during her junior year in high school. As a result, she chose to attend Howard University, where she majored in business management. She earned a master's degree in organizational management from the University of Phoenix.

At Howard University, Camye's favorite business course was Human Resource Management, and the professor for that course became her mentor. When she graduated from college, she became a merchandise buyer for a national retailer in Orlando, Florida. With her ultimate goal in mind, she kept in contact with a college campus recruiter from Walt Disney World because she knew that one day her career would lead to that world-class organization. One day she received a call about an opening. She joined Walt Disney World as an operations manager, transitioned into human resources, and later became a Walt Disney Ambassador representing the company across the world.

After 11 years at Disney, Camye was recruited to become Vice President of Human Resources for Special Olympics International. She worked there with its founder, Eunice Kennedy Shriver, who became a mentor.

When Camye had her second child, she left Special Olympics International. She started her own human resources consulting firm, working with start-up and midsized firms, so that she could spend more time with her growing family.

Once her children were older, Camye returned to corporate America, joining the Hospitality Group of B. F. Saul Company. Today she is Vice President of Human Resources with responsibility for driving results in all key human resource functions, including recruitment, training, performance management, risk management, corporate administration, and general administration for the Hospitality Group.

Camye is married with three children.

NINA MCLEMORE
Founder and CEO, Nina McLemore LLC
Founder and former President,
Liz Claiborne Accessories former member Executive
Committee at Liz Claiborne, Inc.

When Nina McLemore graduated from Louisiana State University with a degree in French and economics, her goal was to be a buyer for a department store with an annual salary of $25,000. At age 27, she had become a divisional merchandise manager with 13 buyers reporting to her in New Orleans. She moved to New York at age 29 to become the Vice President for May Department Stores International, traveling the world to find products for the stores.

Nina realized one day, as she was returning from a trip to Asia, that no one was about to ask her to marry him and she was probably going to have to support herself for the rest of her life. It was time, she decided, to think seriously about making a significant amount of money.

Nina left May Department Stores to found Liz Claiborne Accessories in 1980, which she grew to almost $200 million in revenues. It was highly profitable. She was President of Liz Claiborne Accessories and a member of Liz Claiborne Inc.'s Executive Committee. She had structured a compensation plan that earned her a significant amount of Liz Claiborne stock.

In 1993, she left Liz Claiborne to build her financial expertise and to earn her master of business administration degree from the Columbia University Graduate School of Business. Seeing the growth opportunity in venture capital and the ability to learn how to finance and grow businesses in other industries, Nina cofounded Regent Capital, a private equity firm, which invested in consumer and women-led businesses.

By 2003, Nina recognized that the changes in the women's apparel business, plus the growth in the number of executive women, created an opportunity for a collection of quality clothing for women with a professional executive image. Since then, her mission has been to create designer-quality clothing for professional women who want to be taken seriously when they enter a room, travel extensively, and always look chic and understated. The collection is sold in better specialty stores, directly to women by sales consultants who own their own businesses, and through company-owned stores in selected cities.

Nina believes strongly in contributing to the community, particularly organizations supporting women, children, and the arts. One of the reasons she started her own business, after retiring from 35 years of a fast-paced work schedule, was to be able to give more money to these causes. Her company works closely with many nonprofits and donates part of the profits from special events to these organizations.

Nina served as Chair of the Center for Women's Business Research and Fashion Group International. She is a founding member of the Committee of 200 and Women Corporate Directors. She is a member of the International Women's Forum, the World President's Organization, and the Women President's Organization.

Nina is married to an attorney in Washington, D.C.

KATHLEEN (KATE) A. NEALON
Non-Executive Director at Argo Group International Holdings, Ltd.; Retired Group Head of Legal and Compliance at Standard Chartered Plc.

Kathleen (Kate) Nealon has broken new ground for women throughout her career. She went to Georgetown University the first year that the College of Arts and Sciences accepted women, and then she studied law at the Georgetown Law School. She remembers that only 18 percent of those in her class, the class of 1975, were women.

After her first year in law school, Kate married a young man—also at the law school—whom she had met during her junior year in college. Her interest was international law, and right out of law school she joined a firm doing business with Latin American companies.

During her first year of practice, Kate had her first son. The firm did not have a policy for pregnancy, and neither, for that matter, did any other U.S. company at that time. However, in 1979 the Women's Anti-Pregnancy Discriminatory Act was passed, and pregnancy was now to be treated as a minor disability. Kate's first son was born one month after the law went into effect. Her second child was born three years later. She says it was a little different to have two young children as a lawyer in a big New York City law firm in the late 1970s. Five years later, while still with the same law firm, she had her third child.

After 10 years, she moved to a law firm specializing in Asia. Although the firm's headquarters was in California, she continued to live in New York City, commuting to California and traveling extensively in Asia. Her practice focused on Chinese and Japanese banks, which she enjoyed, and her career focus became transactions and regulatory work of international financial institutions.

Ultimately in 1992, she was hired by one of her clients, Standard Chartered Plc. as Group Head of Legal and Compliance for the Americas, based in New York City. The bank had never had a lawyer in its U.S. operation, so she was the first in that position. In 1996, the bank wanted to promote her to the position of Group Head of Compliance for the corporation. Although the position had traditionally been based in London, she was loath to move because she had only recently found a suitable school for her son, who had been diagnosed with severe dyslexia. After some consideration, the bank agreed to try having her do the job from New York. For two and a half years, she traveled extensively not only to London, but globally to the bank's locations around the world. She was on the road one week a month to distant locations in Asia, Africa, India, and the Middle East.

By then, her son was progressing well, and she and the bank came to the conclusion that it would be better if the job was based in London. So she moved her family to London. Failing to find the right school for her son in central London, she and her husband and four other families founded the first school for dyslexics over the age of 11 in central London, which is still thriving. After two years, she was promoted to Group Head of Legal and Compliance for the corporation and was a member of the bank's Executive Committee. She probably was the first female general counsel at a large European financial institution in 2000.

Health problems required Kate to retire in 2004. However, she was extremely well respected, and the bank sponsored her move onto what is known in the United Kingdom as a portfolio career path. This is a career path for executives at the end of their careers who become candidates for public, often FTSE-traded, boards of directors. Thanks in great part to the support of Standard Chartered Bank, Kate has become one of a group of executives who are part of this pool.

Since 2004, Kate has served as a Non-Executive Director on a number of boards, including Shire Plc., Cable & Wireless Communications Plc., and Argo Group International Holdings, Ltd. In addition, she founded and leads the Georgetown Law School European Law Alumni Advisory

Group, which hosts a legal conference in a different European capital each year.

Kate's nonprofit service includes the Advisory Council of the Institute of Business Ethics; the Finance and Planning Committee, Westminster Cathedral, London; Ambassador for the Well-Being of Women, a women's health charity; the Advisory Board of the Centre for Business Research, Cambridge University; and the Advisory Board of Georgetown Law School.

Kate is married with three children. She holds joint U.S./U.K. citizenship.

USHA PILLAI, PH.D., MS, PMP
Founder and President of Aria Management Consulting, LLC, formerly Senior Director at Pfizer

Usha Pillai remembers that as a child she always wanted to help other people. That led to her desire to go to pharmacy school. She graduated from the Bombay College of Pharmacy in Mumbai, India. Some friends had gone to the United States for their education, and she decided that she too would like to pursue her education there. She earned an executive master's degree in technology management from Rensselaer Polytechnic Institute in Hartford, Connecticut, and a Ph.D. in pharmaceutical sciences from the University of Louisiana. She did postdoctoral work at the University of Arizona.

Thanks to an introduction by a former postdoctoral fellow from the University of Arizona, Usha was offered a position at Pfizer in its newly expanded animal health organization. She eventually became a manager in this division and was involved in three products that made it to the market; however, she wanted to return to her primary love, human health. She also wanted to learn how a company like Pfizer works, so she sought positions that allowed her to move through a variety of business areas. During her 16-year career at Pfizer, she had the opportunity to manage multiple laboratories and to work in leadership and management positions in diverse functions. She gained experience in the areas of intellectual property, strategy management, business development, international sourcing, alliance management, and mergers/acquisitions/integration.

Usha headed global strategic sourcing for the Pharmacokinetics, Dynamics and Metabolism Division, leading a group that was responsible for developing and implementing national and international sourcing strategy. She also was responsible for integration planning for worldwide research during Pfizer's acquisition of King Pharmaceuticals.

Usha applied for and received a Pfizer Global Health Fellowship. She spent six months in Ghana working with a nonprofit organization on malaria education and management. When she returned to work at Pfizer in Connecticut, the positions she was asked to consider did not offer her the growth opportunities she wanted. After several months of discussion and reflection, she decided it was time to leave Pfizer and pursue other opportunities. Pfizer had just purchased King Pharmaceuticals, however, and her vice president asked her to stay on to manage the integration planning for the worldwide research organization, which she did.

Usha says, "It was a great company and a great journey for me. I wouldn't be where I am without the opportunities it afforded me."

Usha's long-term vision is to create a nonprofit health education organization funded by a for-profit company. Toward that goal, she recently founded Aria Management Consulting, LLC, to help companies crystallize their visions into action.

KIM ROBERTS
Director of Government Analysis
Science Applications International Corporation (SAIC)

While in college, Kim Roberts did a congressional internship. During the summer interning in Washington, D.C., she fell in love with politics and policy. This experience influenced the rest of her career. Kim graduated with a bachelor's degree in international politics from Pennsylvania State University and took a job with John Anderson's presidential campaign as an advance person. After the campaign, she decided that a career in journalism would give her the opportunity to combine her love of politics and policy.

Kim talked her way into a job at United Press International (UPI) as a copyeditor, taking dictation over the telephone from field reporters. Kim stayed at UPI Television News (which later became Worldwide Television

News) for 14 years, working her way up to become a television reporter and documentary producer.

Not satisfied with merely watching policy briefings, Kim decided to pursue a master's degree in international public policy at the Johns Hopkins School of Advanced International Studies at night while working full time. The company supported her and assigned her to produce mini-documentaries on the Middle East and elsewhere related to the papers she was writing in school.

Kim's documentaries and reporting have covered the Palestinian Liberation Organization, the emergence of democracy in Jordan, the Middle East peace talks, the Okinawa gubernatorial election, and military intervention in Haiti. She has interviewed PLO chairman Yasser Arafat and Jordan's King Hussein.

After Kim left Worldwide Television News, she worked at Swiss Broadcasting and Associated Press (AP) Television News and did freelancing assignments. She moved to Swiss Television in order to cover the U.S. election for a foreign audience.

While on assignment in Haiti, Kim met her husband, who was in the U.S. Marine Corps. After they married, she made the decision to move with him as his assignments changed. At every duty station, she was creative in finding opportunities to continue building her professional portfolio. When they were in Okinawa, she did freelance work for her former company, Worldwide Television News—traveling to Korea and Tokyo to do economic stories and to do a story on what the Okinawa gubernatorial election meant to Americans. She was offered and accepted the position of U.S. Army Public Affairs Office for Okinawa. As she and her husband changed duty stations, she continued to do freelance assignments. When they returned to the United States, Kim took the opportunity to get her Ph.D. in international studies at the University of Miami.

After her husband retired from the military, Kim and her husband returned to Washington, D.C. She joined Science Applications International Corporation (SAIC) as Director of Government Analysis. She provides policy and public affairs analysis and decision support to senior leaders in government and the private sector.

While her career was not linear in the traditional sense, it was linear in the big-picture sense. She has always pursued a career in political and international affairs as a journalist or through other policy venues.

Kim is married.

JUDITH "JUDY" D. ROBINSON
Colonel, Medical Service Corps
United States Army

Colonel Judith (Judy) Robinson graduated from Luther College in three years with a bachelor's degree in psychobiology and completed the course work for a chemistry major. Following college, she traveled through Central and South American. In Ecuador, she taught science and English, earning enough money that she was able to travel through Europe.

On almost the same day that Judy returned home, the private ambulance service that had been serving the community withdrew, and the mayor asked her to establish and lead a new local service. Since she was planning on applying to graduate school, she agreed to establish and lead the ambulance service while she was going through the application process.

Judy was accepted at the American Graduate School "Thunderbird" College in Arizona, where she earned a master's degree in international management with an emphasis in marketing. She went to New York and worked in international marketing for three years, and then asked herself, "Is that all there is?" At this time, her mother became ill, and she decided to return home to care for her mother. After spending time with her mother, she decided to go back to school and get a master of education degree at Temple University in Philadelphia.

Judy did not come from a military family, but she had always wanted to go into the Army. Before she came home to stay with her mother, she had been exploring going into the military. But, having already managed people and programs and budgets, she did not want to enlist and spend several years working her way up to become an officer. While at Temple University, she found a recruiter who was able to help her apply for a direct commission as an officer. So she was commissioned as a reserve officer and went off to the Officer Basic Course. Her plan had been to stay in the reserves, but when the opportunity presented itself to go on active duty and be stationed in Germany as a platoon leader, she accepted. Twenty-seven years later, she is still in the Regular Army.

Colonel Robinson is a Medical Service Corps officer. She has served at every level from Platoon Leader to Army Staff. Her assignments have included field command positions in Germany, Saudi Arabia (Desert

Shield/Desert Storm), and at Fort Bragg, North Carolina, and Fort Hood, Texas. She was the Garrison Commander at Fort Detrick, Maryland.

In some cases, she was in a job where Army precedent said women were not supposed to be at that time. She helped change the perceptions that came with those precedents.

Today, Colonel Robinson is teaching at the Army War College in Carlisle, Pennsylvania. Along the way, she has added to her academic credentials. She earned a master of strategic studies at the Army War College and did a fellowship in military medical history at the Uniformed Services University of Health Science.

Her awards include a Legion of Merit, Bronze Star Medal, seven Meritorious Service Awards, three Army Commendation Medals, a Joint Service Achievement Medal, and three Army Achievement Medals. She is a member of the College of Contingency Planning, the American Academy of Medical Administrators, the Association of Military Surgeons of the United States, Women in Defense, National Defense Industrial Association, the Order of Saint Barbara, and the Order of Military Medical Merit.

Colonel Robinson has one son and has been a single mother for most of her Army career.

Works Cited

Adler, Roy D. "Women in the Executive Suite Correlate to High Profits." Malibu, CA: Pepperdine University, 2008.

Anderson, Melissa J., Jan. 2, 2011. "Voice of Experience: Fiona O'Hara, Senior Executive Technology DOO, Accenture." *The Glass Hammer*, http://www.theglasshammer.com/news/2012/01/02/voice-of-experience-fiona-ohara.

———, Oct. 20, 2011. "Position Yourself for Success: Female Leaders Share Advice at the 2011 Women on Wall Street Conference." *The Glass Hammer*, http://www.theglasshammer.com/news/2011/10/20/position-yourself-for-success.

———, Dec. 15, 2012. "Movers and Shakers: Karen Wimbish, Director of Retail Retirement, Wells Fargo." *The Glass Hammer*, http://www.theglasshammer.com/news/2011/12/15/movers-and-shakers-ka.

Ante, Spencer E., and Joann S. Lublin. "IBM Names Rometty as Next CEO." *Wall Street Journal*, Oct. 26, 2011.

Auletta, Ken. "A Woman's Place: Can Sheryl Sandberg Upend Silicon Valley's Male-dominated Culture?" *New Yorker*, July 11, 2011, http://www.newyorker.com/reporting/2011/07/11/110711fa_fact_auletta?currentPage=all.

Barsh, Joanna, and Lareina Yee, "Unlocking the Full Potential of Women in the US Economy." *McKinsey & Company*, Apr. 2011, http://www.mckinsey.com/Client_Service/Organization/Latest_thinking/Unlocking_the_full_potential.

Bass, Bernard M. "Two Decades of Research and Development in Transformational Leadership." *European Journal of Work and Organizational Psychology* 1(1999): 9–32.

Beck, Barbara. "Closing the Gap." *The Economist*, Nov. 26, 2011.

Benko, Cathy. "How the Corporate Ladder Became the Corporate Lattice." *Harvard Business Review*, Nov. 4, 2010, http://blogs.hbr.org/cs/2010/11/how_the_corporate_ladder_becam.html.

Bennis, Warren. *On Becoming a Leader*. Boston: Addison-Wesley, 1988; 4th ed., New York: Basic Books, 2009.

Booth, Alison L. "Gender and Competition." *Labour Economics* 16, 2009, 599606. Doi: 10.1016/j.labeco.2009.08.002.

Bryant, Adam. "Distilling the Wisdom of C.E.O.'s, excerpt from *The Corner Office*," *New York Times*, Feb. 16, 2011. http://www.nytimes.com/2011/04/17/business/17excerpt.htmlpagewanted=all.

Cameron, Kim. *Leader to Leader Journal*, Nov. 8, 2011.

Cameron, Kim, and Arran Caza. "Developing Strategies for Responsible Leadership," http://webuser.bus.umich.edu/cameronk/PDFs/Management%20Skills/RESPONSIBLE%20LEADERSHIP%20-%20MAY%20REVISION.pdf.

Carter, Nancy M., and Christine Silva. "Pipeline's Broken Promise," Catalyst, 2009, http://www.catalyst.org/publication/372/pipelines-broken-promise.

Catalyst, 2004. "The Bottom Line: Connecting Corporate Performance and Gender Diversity."

Catalyst, 2011. "The Myth of the Ideal Worker: Does Doing All the Right Things Really Get Women Ahead?"

Catalyst, 2012. "U.S. Women in Business," http://www.catalyst.org/publication/132/us-women-in-business.

Center for Women's Business Research [formerly National Foundation for Women Business Owners], 1999. "Philanthropy among Business Women of Achievement."

———, 2002. "Active and Engaged: The Investment Goals and Strategies of High Net Worth Investors."

———, 2004. "The Leading Edge, Women-owned Million Dollar Firms."

———, 2005. "Capital Choices": Volume One, "What Matters and What Works," Ch.2.2.

Cox, Caroline. "Anne Stevens, Chairman, CEO and Principal, SA IT Services" *Little PINK Book*, http://littlepinkbook.comesurces/pink-profiles/anne-stevens, Dec. 1, 2011.

Cunningham, Lillian. "The Rolodex That Redefined Power." *Washington Post*, Dec. 25, 2011.

Davis, Ian. "Women and Leadership." *The McKinsey Quarterly*, no. 4 (2008).

De Vita, Emma. "Trust and the Female Boss." *MT Management Today*, Sept. 1, 2010, http://www.managementtoday.co.uk/news/1023469/.

Doige, Norman. *The Brain That Changes Itself*. New York: Penguin Group, 2007.

"Fortune's Most Powerful Women Summit," *Fortune*, 2011.

Fox, Tom. "On Leadership: The Federal Coach." *Washington Post*, Feb. 22, 2011.

Groysberg, Boris. "How Star Women Build Portable Skills." *Harvard Business Review*, Feb. 2008, http://hbr.org/2008/02/how-star-women-build-portable-skills/ar/1.

Gurian, Michael, and Barbara Annis. *Leadership and the Sexes, Using Gender Science to Create Success in Business*. Hoboken, NJ: Jossey-Bass, 2008.

Hadary, Sharon. "Perspectives on Leadership and Success: Vision, Values and Lessons Learned from Top Women Executives." *The Committee of 200*, Oct. 2011.

Hegelsen, Sally. *The Female Advantage: Women's Ways of Leadership*. New York: Doubleday Currency, 1990.

Hewlett, Sylvia A., Kerrie Peraino, Laura Sherbin, and Karen Sumberg. "The Sponsor Effect: Breaking through the Last Glass Ceiling." *Harvard Business Review*, Jan. 12, 2011, http://cpradr.org/Portals/0/Committees/Industry%20Committees/National%20Task%20Force%20on%20Diversity%20in%20ADR/Materials/The%20Sponsor%20Effect%20-%20Breaking%20Through%20the%20Last%20Glass%20Ceiling.pdf.

Hewlett, Sylvia A., and Ripa Rashid, "Want to Win the Talent War in Emerging Markets? Start Recruiting Women." *Fast Company*, Aug. 1, 2011, http://www.fastcompany.com/1770789/women-are-the-solution-to-winning-the-war-for-talent-in-emerging-markets?partner=leadership_newsletter.

Javidan, Mansour, Peter W. Dorfman, Mary Sully de Luque, and Robert J. House. "In the Eye of the Beholder: Cross Cultural Lessons in Leadership from Project GLOBE." *Academy of Management Perspectives* 20 (1): 67–90. 2006.

Knapp, Bill. "A Case for Optimism." *Washington Post*, Jan. 16, 2012.

Korn, Melissa. "Dose of Humility with a Harvard MBA." *Wall Street Journal*, Sept. 26, 2011, http://online.wsj.com/article/SB10001424053111904563904576588583893732362.html.

Lalanne, M., and P. Seabright. "Contact Sports: Women Are Worse than Men at Turning Networks to Their Advantage." *The Economist*, Nov. 2011, http://www.economist.comode/138162.

Li, Charlene. "The Failure Imperative." *The Conference Board Review* 2010, http://www.conference-board.org/publications/publication detail.cfm?publicationid=21219bios.docx.

Lubin, Joann S., and Kelly Eggers. "More Woman are Primed to Land CEO Roles," *Wall Street Journal*, April 30, 2012.

Maddox, J. E. "Self-efficacy: The Power of Believing You Can." *Handbook of Positive Psychology*. New York: Oxford University Press. 2002.

"Moving Women to the Top: McKinsey Global Survey Results." *McKinsey Quarterly*, 2010, www.mckinseyquarterly.com/Moving_women_to_the_top_McKinsey_Global_Survey_results_2686.

NASA Goddard Space Flight Center, Clair L. Partingson, Pamela S. Millar, and Michele Thallar, eds., Goddard in Association with the Maryland Women's Heritage Center, "Women of Goddard: Careers in Science, Technology, Engineering, and Mathematics," July 2011.

National Foundation for Women Business Owners (now Center for Women's Business Research). "Leaders in Business and Community, the Philanthropic Contributions of Women and Men Business Owners," Nov. 2000.

"New Study Finds Small Groups Demonstrate Distinctive 'Collective Intelligence' When Facing Difficult Tasks." *MIT Media Relations*, Sept. 30, 2010, http://web.mit.edu/press/2010/collective-intel.html.

Pfeffer, Jeffrey. "Don't Dismiss Office Politics—Teach It." *Wall Street Journal*, Oct. 24, 2011, R6.

Sangster, Elissa E. "Women Must Appreciate the Value of an MBA." *Financial Times*, Nov. 21, 2011, http://www.ft.com/intl/cms/s/2/49c47720 -0eel-11e1-b585-00144feabdc0.html.

Santovec, Mary Lou. "Self-Efficacy Is a Critical Attribute for Women Leaders, *Women in Higher Education* (April 2010): 8.

"Time Inc. Finds Its Future." *Wall Street Journal*, Dec. 1, 2011, http://online .wsj.com/article/SB10001424052970204012004577069971240704762 .html.

"The Top 50 Women in World Business 2011." *Financial Times*, Nov. 15, 2011.

U.S. Department of Commerce Economics and Statistics Administration and Executive Office of the President Office of Management and

Budget. "Women in America: Indications of Social and Economic Well-Being," 2011.

"The US Employment Challenges: Perspectives from Carl Camden and Michael Spence." *McKinsey Quarterly*, Aug. 2011.

Wagner, James. "She's Won Them Over." *Washington Post*, Nov. 24, 2011.

Werhane, Patricia. "Women Leaders in a Globalized World," *Journal of Business Ethics*, (Spring 2007): 425–435.

"Why Women Make Better Investors." *Money*, Jan. 23, 2006.

"Women 'Better Investors Than Men,'" *BBC News*, June 3, 2005.

Women's Philanthropy Institute, Center on Philanthropy at Indiana University, Debra J. Mesch, "Women Give 2010: New Research about Women and Giving," Oct. 2010.

Notes

Introduction: The New World of Women's Leadership

1. "Women in America: Indications of Social and Economic Well-Being." U.S. Department of Commerce Economics and Statistics Administration and Executive Office of the President, Office of Management and Budget (2011).
2. Catalyst, "U.S. Women in Business," http://www.catalyst.org/publication/ 132/us-women-in-business (2012).
3. Ibid.
4. Ibid.
5. Barbara Beck, "Closing the Gap," *The Economist*, Nov. 26, 2011.
6. Ian Davis, "Women and Leadership," *McKinsey Quarterly*, no. 4 (2008).
7. Pepperdine University, Roy D. Adler, "Women in the Executive Suite Correlate to High Profits" (2008).
8. Catalyst, "The Bottom Line: Connecting Corporate Performance and Gender Diversity" (Jan. 2004), http://www. Catalyst.org/publications/ 82/the-bottom-line-connecting-corporate-performance-and-gender -diversity.
9. Davis, "Women and Leadership" (2008).
10. "Moving Women to the Top: McKinsey Global Survey Results," *McKinsey Quarterly* (2010).
11. Catalyst, Nancy M. Carter and Christine Silva, "Pipeline's Broken Promise" (2009), http://www.catalyst.org/publication/372/pipelines -broken-promise.
12. Lillian Cunningham, "The Rolodex That Redefined Power," *Washington Post*, Dec. 25, 2011.

13. Carter and Silva, "Pipeline's Broken Promise."
14. Beck, "Closing the Gap."

Success Strategy One: Empower the Woman Leader Within

1. Melissa J. Anderson, "Voice of Experience: Fiona O'Hara, Senior Executive Technology DOO, Accenture," *The Glass Hammer*, Jan. 2, 2011, http://www.theglasshammer.comews/2012/01/02/voice-of-experience-fiona-ohara.
2. Bernard M. Bass, "Two Decades of Research and Development in Transformational Leadership," *European Journal of Work and Organizational Psychology* 1: 9–32 (1999).
3. "New Study Finds Small Groups Demonstrate Distinctive 'Collective Intelligence' When Facing Difficult Tasks," MIT Media Relations press release, Sept. 30, 2010, available at http://web.mit.edu/press/collective_intel.html.
4. Spencer E. Ante and Joann S. Lublin, "IBM Names Rometty as Next CEO," *Wall Street Journal*, Oct. 26, 2011.
5. Emma De Vita, "Trust and the Female Boss," *MT Management Today*, Sept. 1, 2010, http://www.managementtoday.co.uk/news/1023469/.
6. James Wagner, "She's Won Them Over," *Washington Post*, Nov. 24, 2011.
7. "Time Inc. Finds Its Future in Digital Ad Executive," *Wall Street Journal*, December 1, 2011.
8. Sally Hegelsen, *The Female Advantage: Women's Ways of Leadership* (New York: Doubleday/Currency, 1990).
9. Michael Gurian and Barbara Annis, *Leadership and the Sexes, Using Gender Science to Create Success in Business* (San Francisco: Jossey-Bass, 2008).
10. Ibid.
11. Ibid.
12. Ibid.
13. Norman Doige, *The Brain That Changes Itself* (New York: Penguin Group, 2007).
14. Lillian Cunningham, "The Rolodex That Redefined Power," *Washington Post*, Dec. 25, 2011.
15. Anderson, "Voice of Experience: Fiona O'Hara."
16. Patricia Werhane, "Women Leaders in a Globalized World," *Journal of Business Ethics* 74:425–435 (2007).

Success Strategy Two: Own Your Destiny

1. Alison L. Booth, "Gender and Competition," Labour Economics 16 (2009), 599–600, doi: 1016/j.labco.2009. http://www.sciencedirect .com/science/journal/09275371/16.

2. Sharon Hadary, "Perspectives on Leadership and Success: Vision, Values and Lessons Learned from Top Women Executives," *The Committee of 200* (Oct. 2011).

3. Mary Lou Santovec, "Self-Efficacy Is a Critical Attribute for Women Leaders, *Women in Higher Education*, Issue 44 (Apr. 2010): 8.

4. J. E. Maddox, "Self-Efficacy: The Power of Believing You Can," *Handbook of Positive Psychology* (New York: Oxford University Press,).

5. Melissa J. Anderson, "Voice of Experience: Fiona O'Hara, Senior Executive Technology DOO, Accenture," *The Glass Hammer*, Jan. 2, 2011, available at http://www.theglasshammer.comews/2012/01/02/ voice-of-experience-fiona-ohara.

6. Charlene Li, "The Failure Imperative," *The Conference Board Review* (July 2010), http/www.tcbreview.com/the-failure-imperative.php.

7. www.WomansAdvantage.biz.

8. "The Top 50 Women in World Business 2011," *Financial Times*, Nov. 15, 2011, www.ft.com/cms/s/0/68e02aa0-0f18-11e1-b585-00144feabdc0 .html.

9. Center for Women's Business Research, *Capital Choices: Volume 1, What Matters and What Works*, Ch. 2.2 (2005).

10. NASA Goddard Space Flight Center, Clair L. Partinson, Pamela S. Millar, and Michelle Thallar, eds., Goddard in Association with the Maryland Women's Heritage Center (MWHC), "Women of Goddard: Careers in Science, Technology, Engineering, and Mathematics" (July 2011).

11. Hadary, "Perspectives on Leadership and Success."

12. NASA Goddard Space Flight Center, 2011.

13. Warren Bennis, *On Becoming a Leader* (Boston: Addison-Wesley, 1989; 4th ed., New York: Basic Books, 2009).

14. Caroline Cox, "Anne Stevens, Chairman, CEO and Principal, SA IT Services," *Little PINK Book*, http://littlepinkbook.com/resources/pink -profiles/anne-stevens.

15. Melissa J. Anderson, "Movers and Shakers: Karen Wimbish, Director of Retail Retirement, Wells Fargo," *The Glass Hammer* (Dec. 15, 2012), http/www.theglasshammer.com/news011/12/15/movers-and -shakers-ka.

16. "The US Employment Challenges: Perspectives from Carl Camden and Michael Spence," *McKinsey Quarterly* (Aug. 2011), available at http://www.mckinseyquarterly.com/The_US_employment_challenge_ Perspectives_from_Carl_Camden_and_Michael_Spence_2849.

Success Strategy Three: Be the Architect of Your Career

1. Joanna Barsh and Lareina Yee, "Unlocking the Full Potential of Women in the US Economy," *McKinsey & Company* (Apr. 2011), http:// www.mckinsey.com/Client_Service/Organization/Latest_thinking/ Unlocking_the_full potential.aspx.

2. Melissa J. Anderson, "Movers and Shakers: Karen Wimbish, Director of Retail Retirement, Wells Fargo," *The Glass Hammer*, Dec. 15, 2012, http://www.theglasshammer.com/news/2011/12/15/movers-and -shakers-karenwimbish-director-of-retail-retirement-wells-fargo/.

3. Ken Auletta, "A Woman's Place: Can Sheryl Sandberg Upend Silicon Valley's Male-Dominated Culture?" *New Yorker*, July 11, 2011, http://www.newyorker.com/reporting/2011/07/11/110711fa_fact_ auletta?currentPage=all.

4. Joann S. Lubin and Kelly Eggers, "More Women Are Primed to Land CEO Roles," *Wall Street Journal*, April 30, 2012.

5. Melissa Korn, "Dose of Humility with a Harvard MBA," *Wall Street Journal*, Sept. 25, 2011, available at http://online.wsj.com/article/SB10 0014240531119045639045765885883893732362.html.

6. Sylvia A. Hewlett and Ripa Rashid, "Want to Win the Talent War in Emerging Markets? Start Recruiting Women," *Fast Company* (Aug. 1, 2011), available at http://www.fastcompany.com/1770789/ women-are-the-solution-to-winning-the-war-for-talent-in-emerging -markets?partner=leadership_newsletter.

7. Mansour Javidan, Peter W. Dorfman, Mary Sully de Luque, and Robert J. House, "In the Eye of the Beholder: Cross Cultural Lessons in Leadership from Project GLOBE," *Academy of Management Perspectives*, 20 (1), 67–90 (Feb. 2006).

8. Elissa E. Sangster, "Women Must Appreciate the Value of an MBA," *Financial Times*, Nov. 21, 2011, http://www.ft.com/intl/cms/s/2/ 49c47720-0eel-11e1-b585-00144feabdco.html.

9. Bill Knapp, "A Case for Optimism," *Washington Post*, Jan. 16, 2012.

10. Cathy Benko, "How the Corporate Ladder Became the Corporate Lattice," *Harvard Business Review*, Nov. 4, 2010, available at http://blogs.

hbr.org/cs/2010/11/how_the_corporate_ladder_becam.html.

11. "Fortune's Most Powerful Women Summit," *Fortune*, 2011, available at http://fortuneconferences.com/mpws2011/.

12. Boris Groysberg, "How Star Women Build Portable Careers," *Harvard Business Review*, Feb. 2008, available at http://hbr.org/2008/02/how -star-women-build-portable-skills/ar/1.

Success Strategy Four: Advocate Unabashedly for Yourself

1. Catalyst, Nancy M. Carter and Christine Silva, "The Myth of the Ideal Worker: Does Doing All the Right Things Really Get Women Ahead?" (2011). Available at http://www.catalyst.org/publication/509/ the-myth-of-the-ideal-worker-does-doing-all-the-right-things-really -get-women-ahead.

2. Melissa J. Anderson, "Position Yourself for Success: Female Leaders Share Advice at the 2011 Women on Wall Street Conference," *The Glass Hammer* (Oct. 20, 2011), available at http://www.theglasshammer.com/news/2011/10/20/position-yourself-for-success.

3. Center for Women's Business Research, "The Leading Edge: Women-Owned Million Dollar Firms" (2004), available at http://www. womensbusinessresearchcenter.org/publications/pubsforpurchase/ theleadingedgewome/.

4. Jeffrey Pfeffer, "Don't Dismiss Office Politics—Teach It," *Wall Street Journal*, Oct. 24, 2011, R6.

5. M. Lalanne and P. Seabright, "Contact Sports: Women Are Worse than Men at Turning Networks to Their Advantage," *The Economist*, Nov. 2011, available at http://www.economist.comode/138162.

6. Sylvia A. Hewlett, Kerrie Peraino, Laura Sherbin, and Karen Sumberg, "The Sponsor Effect: Breaking through the Last Glass Ceiling," *Harvard Business Review*, Jan. 12, 2011, available at http://cpradr.org/ Portals/0/Committees/Industry%20Committees/National%20 Task%20Force%20on%20Diversity%20in%20ADR/Materials/The%20 Sponsor%20Effect%20-%20Breaking%20Through%20the%20 Last%20Glass%20Ceiling.pdf.

7. Ibid.

8. Ibid.

9. Ibid.

10. Ibid.

Success Strategy Six: Create Exceptional Teams

1. Adam Bryant," Distilling the Wisdom of C.E.O.'s," excerpt from *The Corner Office, New York Times*, April 16, 2011, available at http://www.nytimes.com/2011/04/17/business/17excerpt.html?_r=1&pagewanted=all.

2. Melissa J. Anderson, "Position Yourself for Success: Female Leaders Share Advice at the 2011 Women on Wall Street Conference," *The Glass Hammer* (Oct. 20, 2011), available at http://www.theglasshammer.com/news/2011/10/20/position-yourself-for-success-female-leaders-share-advice-at-the-2011-women-on-wall-street-conference.

3. Caroline Cox, "Anne Stevens, Chairman, CEO and Principal, SA IT Services," *Little PINK Book*, Dec. 1, 2011, available at http://littlepink book.com/resources/pink-profiles/anne-stevens.

4. Kim Cameron, excerpted from *Leader to Leader Journal*, Nov. 8, 2011, available at http://www.leadersofthenewcentury.com.

5. Kim Cameron and Arran Caza, "Developing Strategies for Responsible Leadership," available at http://webuser.bus.umich.edu/cameronk/PDFs/Management%20Skills/RESPONSIBLE%20LEADERSHIP%20-%20MAY%20REVISION.pdf

6. Ibid.

7. Robert Sutton, "How a Few Bad Apples Ruin Everything," *Wall Street Journal*, Oct. 24, 2011, available at http://online.wsj.com/article/SB10001424052970203499704576622550325233260.html.

Success Strategy Seven: Nurture Your Greatest Asset—You

1. Tom Fox, "On Leadership: the Federal Coach," *Washington Post*, Feb. 22, 2011.

2. Ken Auletta, "A Woman's Place: Can Sheryl Sandberg Upend Silicon Valley's Male-dominated Culture?" *The New Yorker*, July 11, 2011, available at http://www.newyorker.com/reporting/2011/07/11/110711fa_fact_auletta?currentPage=all.

3. Ibid.

4. Adam Bryant, "Distilling the Wisdom of C.E.O.'s," excerpt from *The Corner Office, New York Times*, April 16, 2011, available at http://www.nytimes.com/2011/04/17/business/17excerpt.html?_r=1&pagewanted=all.

5. Center for Women's Business Research, "Active and Engaged: The Investment Goals and Strategies of High Net Worth Investors" (2002).

6. "Why Women Make Better Investors," *Money*, Jan. 23, 2006.

7. "Women Better Investors than Men," *BBC News* (June 3, 2005), available at http//news.bbc.uk/2/hi/business/4600663i.stm.

Success Strategy Eight: Turn Possibilities into Reality
1. Melissa J. Anderson, "Position Yourself for Success: Female Leaders Share Advice at the 2011 Women on Wall Street Conference," (*The Glass Hammer*) Oct. 20, 2011, available at http://www.theglasshammer. com/news/2011/10/20/position-yourself-for-success-female-leaders -share-advice-at-the-2011-women-on-wall-street-conference.
2. Women's Philanthropy Institute, Center on Philanthropy at Indiana University, Debra J. Mesch, Ph.D. and Director, "Women Give 2010: New Research about Women and Giving" (Oct. 2010), available at http://www.womenscolleges.org/files/pdfs/womengive2010report.pdf.
3. National Foundation for Women Business Owners (now Center for Women's Business Research), "Leaders in Business and Community, the Philanthropic Contributions of Women and Men Business Owners" (Nov. 2000).
4. National Foundation for Women Business Owners, "Philanthropy among Businesswomen of Achievement" (Nov. 1999).

Index